PEARSON LONGMAN

KEYSTONE

D

PEARSON English Learning System

Workbook

Anna Uhl Chamot

John De Mado

Sharroky Hollie

PEARSON

Upper Saddle River, New Jersey • Boston, Massachusetts • Chandler, Arizona • Glenview, Illinois

PEARSON LONGMAN
KEYSTONE

D

PEARSON English Learning System

Workbook

Staff credits: The people who made up the *Longman Keystone* team, representing editorial, production, design, manufacturing, and marketing, are John Ade, Rhea Banker, Liz Barker, Danielle Belfiore, Virginia Bernard, Kenna Bourke, Anne Boynton-Trigg, Jeffrey Buckner, Johnnie Farmer, Patrice Fraccio, Charles Green, Henry Hild, David L. Jones, Lucille M. Kennedy, Ed Lamprich, Emily Lippincott, Tara Maceyak, Maria Pia Marrella, Linda Moser, Laurie Neaman, Sherri Pemberton, Liza Pleva, Joan Poole, Edie Pullman, Tania Saiz-Sousa, Chris Siley, Lynn Sobotta, Jennifer Stem, Jane Townsend, Marian Wassner, Lauren Weidenman, and Adina Zoltan.

Smithsonian American Art Museum contributors: Project director and writer: Elizabeth K. Eder, Ph.D.; Writer: Mary Collins; Image research assistants: Laurel Fehrenbach, Katherine G. Stilwill, and Sally Otis; Rights and reproductions: Richard H. Sorensen and Leslie G. Green; Building photograph by Tim Hursley.

Cover Image: Background, John Foxx/Getty Images; Inset, José Ortega/Images.com
Text composition: TSI Graphics
Text font: 11 pt ITC Stone Sans Std
Photos: 9, Digital Vision/Getty Images; 11, SW Productions/Photodisc/Getty Images; 11, Dorling Kindersley; 14, Hideo Kurihara/Alamy Images; 21, Cyril Furlan/Stock Connection; 22, Lewis W. Hine/George Eastman House/Hulton Archive/Getty Images; 25, Lewis Wickes Hine/CORBIS; 28, Mary Kate Denny/PhotoEdit; 47, Clive Boursnell/Dorling Kindersley; 55, Ken Fisher/Stone Allstock/Getty Images; 61, Stockbyte/Getty Images; 68, Walter Hodges/Taxi/Getty Images; 94, Shutterstock; 127, American Foundation for the Blind, Inc.; 141, Shutterstock; 148, Trinette Reed/Getty Images; 167, Shutterstock; 174, Martin Rogers/Stone Allstock/Getty Images; 181, Robert W. Ginn/PhotoEdit; 207, Rick Friedman/CORBIS; 214, Theo Allofs/Image Bank/Getty Images; 228, C.W.U. Chimpanzee and Human Communication Institute.
Illustrations: Val Paul Taylor, 7; Carol Heyer, 87; Lin Wang, 101; Dusan Petricic, 134; Ron Himler, 188
Technical art: TSI Graphics

ISBN-13: 978-1-4284-3508-7
ISBN-10: 1-4284-3508-5

Printed in the United States of America

13   17

Contents

Unit 1

READING 1

READING 2

READING 3

READING 4

READING 5

Unit 2

Unit 3

READING 1

READING 2

READING 3

READING 4

READING 5

Contents

Unit 4

READING 1

READING 2

READING 3

READING 4

READING 5

Contents

Unit 5

READING 1

READING 2

READING 3

READING 4

READING 5

Unit 6

READING 1

READING 2

READING 3

READING 4

READING 5

TEST PREPARATION

Contents

What is light?

READING 1: "Grandmother Spider Brings the Sun"

VOCABULARY   **Literary Words** *Use with textbook page 5.*

> **REMEMBER** Storytellers use **onomatopoeia** and **repetition** to appeal to your sense of hearing. **Onomatopoeia** is the use of words such as *buzz* which imitate sounds. **Repetition** is using words more than once, such as *long, long, long ago*. **Irony** is the difference between what happens and what is expected to happen in a story.

Decide if the sentences use onomatopoeia, repetition, or irony. Circle the correct choices.

Example: She jingled the change in her pocket and asked for a soda.

(onomatopoeia)   repetition   irony

1. While we were talking, we heard the ding dong of the doorbell.

   onomatopoeia   repetition   irony

2. We knew each other many, many, many years ago.

   onomatopoeia   repetition   irony

3. In the fable "The Lion and the Mouse," the big, strong lion needs the little mouse's help.

   onomatopoeia   repetition   irony

Read the poem. Circle examples of onomatopoeia and underline examples of repetition.

> ## Music Everyday
>
> Oh what a <u>rainy, rainy, rainy</u> night.
> Listen to the (howl) of the wind.
> Or the noise of nearby thunderclaps: krakathoom!
> The sound when our windowpanes rattle and shatter
> Bang and clang and sometimes kaboom,
> Listen, listen, listen to the pitter-pat of rain,
> The everyday music is playing, playing, playing again.

Read the paragraph below. Pay attention to the underlined academic words.

In ancient Native American culture, myths helped explain mysteries of the natural world. We don't know the original author of most Native American myths. Until recently, these stories didn't exist as text. They were told from memory, and passed down from one generation to the next. Storytelling was and is an important tradition for Native Americans.

Write the academic words from the paragraph above next to their correct definitions.

Example: _____culture_____: the art, literature, music, beliefs, and practices of a particular group of people

1. _____: the words in a printed piece of writing

2. _____: a belief, custom, or way of doing something that has existed for a long time

3. _____: someone who writes a book, story, article, or play

Use the academic words from the exercise above to complete the sentences.

4. The _____ of this story has many difficult words.

5. My favorite holiday _____ is the big meal my family enjoys on Thanksgiving.

6. In Cherokee _____ it's important to respect the natural world.

7. I am the _____ of a book of short stories.

Complete the sentences with your own ideas.

Example: The text of that story is ___exciting___ and ___interesting___.

8. One tradition in my family is _____.

9. My favorite author _____ wrote

_____.

10. The thing I like best about American culture is _____.

WORD STUDY **Compound Words** *Use with textbook page 7.*

> **REMEMBER** A compound word is made up of two or more words. Compound words can be written as one word, as in *suntan*. They can be written as two separate words, as in *school bus*. They can be written with a hyphen, as in *sister-in-law*. Check the compound word in a dictionary if you are not sure how it is formed.

Read the compound words in the box below. Then write each compound word in the correct column in the chart.

~~dragonfly~~	health care	able-bodied	voice mail	anybody
waiting room	far-flung	time saver	outlaw	school day
word-of-mouth	blackberry	weekday	red-hot	one-sided

One Word Compound	Hyphenated Compound	Two Word Compound
dragonfly		

Create compound words by combining words. Check your work in a dictionary to see if the compound word is written as one word, separate words, or a hyphenated word.

Example: _____ *week + end = weekend* _____

egg	work	shell	day	in	flow	depth	law	beater

1. _____

2. _____

3. _____

4. _____

5. _____

6. _____

REMEMBER When you read, try to predict by asking "What will happen next?" When you predict, look for clues in the title, story, and illustrations. Also think about what you already know about the topic.

Read the paragraphs. Underline the clues used to make predictions. Then answer the questions.

1. Lola and Brian were lost. "We have to find a way out of the park so we can get home," Brian said. "But how?" asked Lola. They looked for signs to help them, but couldn't find any. Then they saw a policeman walk by.

   What do you think will happen next?

   _____

2. It was the morning of the big math test. Jaime was nervous. He had studied all week long. Sally was even more nervous. She hadn't studied at all. The teacher said, "I hope everyone studied hard. This is the hardest test I've ever given."

   What do you think will happen next?

   _____

3. A group of settlers set out for California. They heard that there was gold in the ground there. When they reached California, they bought shovels.

   What do you think will happen next?

   _____

4. In the morning I made some paintings in Art class. At lunch, I took the paintings outside to the picnic tables to show to my friends. When the bell rang, I ran inside and left them on the table. Later, I looked out the window and saw lightning and heard thunder.

   What do you think will happen next?

   _____

5. Tim had to give a presentation about his family's cultural traditions for a class assignment. He asked his family for help. Tim's grandfather said that passing down stories to family and friends was an important part of their culture.

   What do you think will happen next?

   _____

Name _____ Date _____

COMPREHENSION *Use with textbook page 14.*

Choose the best answer for each item. Circle the letter of the correct answer.

1. All the animals lived on the side of the world that was always _____.

   a. dark   **b.** light   **c.** rainy

2. Possum tried to steal some sun but it _____.

   a. burned his claws   **b.** burned his tail   **c.** escaped from him

3. Buzzard lost his _____ when he tried to steal some sun.

   a. voice   **b.** beak   **c.** feathers

4. Grandmother Spider put the sun in a _____.

   a. clay bowl   **b.** spiderweb   **c.** black bag

5. One thing the story does *not* explain is _____.

   a. why the animals want sun   **b.** how the sun got in the sky   **c.** why the coyote is called the trickster

RESPONSE TO LITERATURE *Use with textbook page 15.*

Myths such as "Grandmother Spider Brings the Sun" were used by people long ago to explain how nature works. Reread pages 12 and 13 of "Grandmother Spider Brings the Sun." Then write a new ending to the story. Your ending should give a different explanation for why the center of a spider's web is always in the shape of a circle.

_____

_____

_____

_____

_____

_____

Unit 1 • Reading 1   **5**

Copyright © by Pearson Education, Inc.

Order of Adjectives *Use with textbook page 16.*

> **REMEMBER** Adjectives are words that describe people, places, and things. When you use more than one adjective before a noun, you must put the adjectives in this order: opinion, size, age, color, and material.

Complete the lists with words from the box.

| purple | wood | yellow | huge | metal |
| tiny | wonderful | weird | young | middle-aged |

Opinion	Size	Age	Color	Material
strange	little	new	blue	clay
kind	large	old	green	cotton
_____	_____	_____	_____	_____
_____	_____	_____	_____	_____

Complete the sentences with the adjectives in parentheses. Write the adjectives in the correct order.

1. (little, strange) The dancing man wore a _____ _____ hat.

2. (white, big) The sailors waved a _____ _____ flag.

3. (brown, old, angry) Inside the cave an _____ _____ _____ bear was resting.

4. (gray, metal, scary, big) They were being chased by a _____ _____ _____ _____ robot!

5. (silk, red, beautiful, new) She put on her _____ _____ _____ _____ shoes.

WRITING

Describe a Character *Use with textbook page 17.*

This is the chart that Evan completed before writing his paragraph.

Physical traits	Character traits
little round animal	shy
cute chubby cheeks	quiet
sharp claws	brave
bushy tail	valiant

Complete your own chart about a character you know from a story.

Physical traits	Character traits

7

UNIT 1

What is light?

READING 2: "Light"

VOCABULARY **Key Words** *Use with textbook page 19.*

Write each word in the box next to its definition.

| concave | convex | opaque | translucent | transparent | wavelength |

Example: *translucent* : clear enough for some light to pass through

1. _____ : the distance between two waves of energy

2. _____ : curved inward like a bowl

3. _____ : clear and easy to see through

4. _____ : curved toward the outside

5. _____ : no light passes through it

Use the words in the box at the top of the page to complete the sentences.

6. A _____ bowl curves inward.

7. No light can pass through a steel door because it is _____ .

8. You can see clearly through a _____ window.

9. A _____ lamp shade curves outward.

10. You can partly see through a _____ curtain.

VOCABULARY Academic Words *Use with textbook page 20.*

Read the paragraph below. Pay attention to the underlined academic words.

> Like heat, light is a form of <u>energy</u>. Objects reflect light, which makes them <u>visible</u> to our eyes. Our eyes <u>interpret</u> different wavelengths of light as colors. Light can travel through some objects. For example, clear glass can <u>transmit</u> light. Some objects, such as mirrors, reflect light in a special way so that you see a <u>virtual</u> image.

Match each word with its definition.

Example: ___*e*___ virtual

_____ **1.** visible

_____ **2.** energy

_____ **3.** transmit

_____ **4.** interpret

a. usable power

b. explain or decide what something means

c. able to be seen

d. pass something through

e. able to be seen but not real

Use the academic words from the exercise above to complete the sentences.

Example: Heat is a form of _____*energy*_____.

5. Your mind can _____ different wavelengths of light as different colors.

6. Large objects are _____ even from far away.

7. The painting shows a _____ image.

8. You can't _____ light through stone or brick.

Complete the sentences with your own ideas.

Example: Your brain interprets wavelengths of light as _____*colors*_____.

9. A _____ and a _____ are visible from where I'm sitting.

10. _____ is a form of energy.

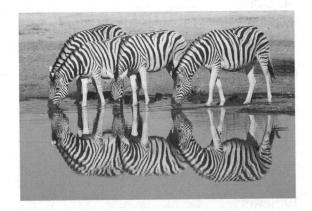

REMEMBER In English, many words end in -*le* as in *thimble* or -*el* as in *gavel*. These last two letters stand for the /əl/ sound. Learning how to spell words with the /əl/ sound can help you spell many words correctly.

Read the words in the box below. Then write the words in the correct column in the chart.

sample	unravel	travel	divisible	gravel
marvel	pickle	tickle	tunnel	example

-*le* words	-*el* words

Write the letter-sound pattern in each word below. Write the definition of each word.

Example: shrivel _____-el_____ *become smaller, wrinkled, and dry*

1. novel _____ _____

2. tremble _____ _____

3. belittle _____ _____

4. sickle _____ _____

5. cruel _____ _____

6. startle _____ _____

7. funnel _____ _____

8. stifle _____ _____

9. satchel _____ _____

10. jewel _____ _____

10

Name _____ Date _____

REMEMBER When you skim a text, you get an understanding of what the text is about. To skim, look at the title, images, and captions. Read the paragraphs quickly and skip over words you don't know.

Skim the article. Then answer the questions that follow.

How Mirrors Work

When you look in a mirror, you see a reflection of yourself. How does this happen?

A mirror reflects light rays smoothly and evenly. That is how a mirror produces an image that looks just like the actual thing it is reflecting.

A mirror is a sheet of glass that has a smooth, silver-colored coating on one side. Glass is transparent, so light passes through it. The silver coating reflects the light rays.

Reflection
Look at this picture. The light rays from the dancer hit the mirror. The mirror reflects the light rays back toward the dancer's eyes. The brain interprets the rays as coming from behind the mirror.

Dancer   Plane mirror   Image

1. Circle the first thing you looked at when you began to skim this article.

2. What did you learn from the images and captions?

   _____

3. Skim the first two paragraphs. What is the general topic of the article?

   _____

4. Read the last paragraph quickly. Write a sentence explaining what the article is about.

   _____

Choose the best answer for each item. Circle the letter of the correct answer.

1. The only part of the electromagnetic spectrum that people can see is _____.

   a. visible light   **b.** ultraviolet rays   **c.** infrared rays

2. Objects can be translucent, opaque, or _____.

   a. transmitted   **b.** reflected   **c.** transparent

3. Diffuse reflection causes light to be _____.

   a. scattered   **b.** opaque   **c.** regular

4. When you look into a plane mirror, you see a _____.

   a. curved image   **b.** virtual image   **c.** diffuse reflection

5. Your image would look bigger in a _____.

   a. convex mirror   **b.** concave mirror   **c.** plane mirror

EXTENSION   *Use with textbook page 29.*

Research five different kinds of electromagnetic waves. Write them in the chart below in order from shortest wavelength to longest.

	Electromagnetic Waves
Short ↑	*gamma rays*
Long ↓	

GRAMMAR

Adverb Clauses of Time *Use with textbook page 30.*

> **REMEMBER** Adverb clauses can be used to show time relationships. They are called adverb clauses of time or time clauses. Each adverb clause of time must be attached to a main clause. When an adverb clause of time comes before the main clause, put a comma after the adverb clause.

Read the sentences. Underline the adverb clauses of time. Circle the main clauses.

Example: <u>Before you leave for school,</u> (make sure you have your books).

1. Whenever you travel, take your passport.

2. I have been emailing her since Tuesday.

3. I played soccer after school.

4. I won't speak to you again until tomorrow.

5. While we were talking, our friends were studying.

Write sentences using the adverb clauses of time in parentheses. Be sure to add commas after the adverb clauses of time when they come before the main clauses.

Example: (before I go to sleep) *Before I go to sleep, I brush my teeth.*

6. (when we talk) _____

7. (after lunch) _____

8. (since this morning) _____

9. (whenever we travel) _____

10. (while we work) _____

11. (until we finish) _____

12. (after school) _____

13. (before I eat) _____

14. (while I do my homework) _____

15. (when you try hard) _____

WRITING

Describe an Object *Use with textbook page 31.*

This is the sensory details chart that Micah completed before writing his paragraph.

Sensory Details	
Sight	*shapes and colors arranged in patterns, bits of colored glass, symmetrical image*
Hearing	*soft swishing sounds as bits of glass move*
Touch	*smooth*
Smell	
Taste	

Complete your own sensory details chart about an object. Appeal to at least two senses.

Sensory Details	
Sight	
Hearing	
Touch	
Smell	
Taste	

UNIT 1 — What is light?

READING 3: "A Game of Light and Shade"

VOCABULARY **Literary Words** *Use with textbook page 33.*

> **REMEMBER** **Imagery** is descriptive language that appeals to the senses. Writers use sensory details to help you see, hear, touch, smell, or taste what the author is describing. The **setting** is the time and place of the action in a literary work.

Read the poem. Circle the examples of imagery.

> In the dawn,
> Creeping across the soft carpet of pine needles
> In bare dancing feet,
> I hear a pretty song: two blue birds
> Carried on warm spring air.
> And hiding beneath a huge and ancient tree
> I sang along.

Based on the clues in the poem, what do you think the setting is?

Place: _____ Time: _____

Write sentences with imagery to describe the settings in parentheses.

Example: (a desert) *The sun beat down on the bright white sands.*

1. (your classroom) _____

2. (the ocean) _____

3. (the moon) _____

4. (your bedroom) _____

5. (a mountain range) _____

Read the paragraph below. Pay attention to the underlined academic words.

Last summer I attended a small art show in Mexico. Seeing so many beautiful paintings was a <u>visual</u> treat. My favorite painting was of a beach at sunset. As I <u>approached</u> the painting, I admired the beautiful colors the artist used. The price of the painting in pesos was the <u>equivalent</u> of about 50 U.S. dollars. <u>Despite</u> the fact that I only had 45 dollars, the artist sold it to me anyway.

Write academic words from the paragraph above next to their correct definitions.

Example: _____*despite*_____: in spite of; regardless of

1. _____: something that has the same value or importance

2. _____: moved closer to

3. _____: relating to seeing or sight

Use academic words from the exercise above to complete the sentences.

4. I went to the party _____ being sick.

5. Painting and sculpture are _____ arts.

6. I _____ the teacher to ask a question.

7. One dime is the _____ of two nickels.

Complete the sentences with your own ideas.

Example: One dollar is the equivalent of _____*ten dimes*_____.

8. I was able to _____ despite being _____.

9. My favorite visual arts are _____ and _____.

10. I approached _____ in order to _____.

Name _____ Date _____

REMEMBER Antonyms are words that have opposite or nearly opposite meanings. For example, *play* is an antonym for *work*. Many words have more than one antonym, so check a dictionary to make sure that the antonym you choose has the exact meaning you need.

Look at the chart below. Write an antonym for each word in the chart.

Words	Antonym
Example: cold	*hot*
1. weak	
2. sluggish	
3. tidy	
4. intelligent	
5. gloomy	

Look at the chart below. Write an antonym for each word. Then write a sentence using the antonym.

Word	Antonym	Sentence
Example: shiny	*dull*	*The silver was dull, not bright.*
6. worthless		
7. heartless		
8. delayed		
9. comfortable		
10. light		

REMEMBER To visualize means to picture a story in your mind. Making these mental images helps you understand the story more clearly.

Read the paragraphs. Underline details that help you to visualize the scenes.

1. "Coming up the stairs you may have noticed how light and sun pour into the tower through the narrow windows. One can feel the change—the cool staircase suddenly becomes quite warm, even in winter. Up here behind the raised stone there is shade. There is no place so good as this for feeling the contrast between light and shade."

2. Pu-Yi zipped her jacket up as high as it would go. The cold mountain wind whipped across her cheeks. Her pack was heavy and her feet crunched in the snow each time she took a step. She looked down to the valley below, and then started to walk up the mountain again.

Read the following paragraph. Underline details that help you visualize the scene. Then answer the questions.

3. Philip covered his eyes as he stepped off the bus. He had never been to a desert town like this. A dry dusty wind blew across the street, and the sun bore down on his soft, young face. He saw a bird circling overhead—it looked like a buzzard. The faint smell of dead flowers drifted on the wind to Philip's nose. He wiped some sweat from his forehead with a handkerchief his mother had given him. Philip kicked dust from his new boots, put a hand through his black hair, and walked into the bank

4. Which senses do these details engage?

   _____

   _____

5. Try to visualize Philip. What details help you to picture what age he is?

   _____

   _____

COMPREHENSION   *Use with textbook page 40.*

Choose the best answer for each item. Circle the letter of the correct answer.

1. The narrator is surprised to find that the man is _____.

   a. deaf   **b.** blind   **c.** alone

2. The narrator follows the man because the narrator is _____.

   a. annoyed   **b.** curious   **c.** angry

3. The man enjoys feeling the contrast of _____.

   a. noise and silence   **b.** happiness and sadness   **c.** sunlight and shade

4. The story is set during the _____.

   a. winter   **b.** spring   **c.** summer

5. The narrator leaves the man feeling _____.

   a. puzzled   **b.** surprised   **c.** glad

RESPONSE to LITERATURE   *Use with textbook page 41.*

Find a paragraph or scene that you like very much in the story. Draw a picture illustrating the images it represents.

Prepositions of Place: *in, at,* and *on* Use with textbook page 42.

REMEMBER The prepositions *in, at,* and *on* can be used to indicate place. Use *in* for countries, states, cities, and places that enclose us. Use *at* for complete addresses and to show something that is at a particular point. Use *on* for the names of streets and to show something that is on a surface.

Each phrase in the box requires one of the prepositions *in, at,* or *on.* Complete the chart with phrases from the box.

Sunset Boulevard	the roof	1600 Pennsylvania Ave.	the living room	San Diego

in	at	on
Tibet	253 Commonwealth Ave.	Newbury St.
the dining room	5 Main St.	the table

Complete the sentences with *in, at,* or *on.*

Example: Dinner is _____ *on* _____ the table.

1. My apartment is _____ the second floor.

2. We went sightseeing _____ Italy.

3. It's dark _____ the closet.

4. The dog lay _____ the carpet.

5. Bill's house is _____ 34 Rolling Terrace Drive.

6. We put the flowers _____ the table.

7. They wanted to meet _____ the restaurant.

8. The table is _____ the kitchen.

9. Please put it back _____ the shelf.

10. Who lives _____ that address?

Name _____ Date _____

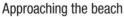

Describe a Place *Use with textbook page 43.*

This is the graphic organizer that Ruth completed before writing her paragraph.

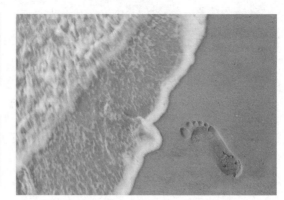

Approaching the beach
busy street, burning hot sand, seagull, rumble of the surf

↓

Standing at the water's edge
cool wet sand, sand dries up, the next wave hits salty air

↓

In the water
feel ecstatic, sun kisses your cheeks, want to stay for as long as you live

Complete your own graphic organizer about a favorite place.

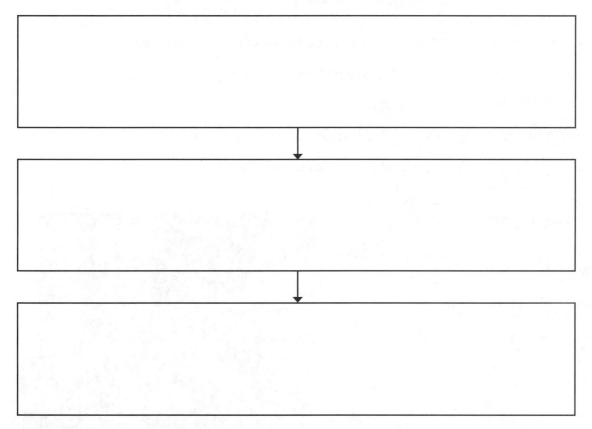

What is light?

READING 4: From *The Eye of Conscience*

VOCABULARY **Key Words** *Use with textbook page 45.*

Write each word in the box next to its definition.

conditions	equipment	immigrants	industrial	inhumanity	miserable

Example: _industrial_: relating to the production of goods, especially in factories

1. _____: the tools and machines needed for an activity

2. _____: very unhappy

3. _____: people who enter another country to live there

4. _____: the situation in which someone lives or something happens

5. _____: cruel treatment of people

Use the words in the box at the top of the page to complete the sentences.

Example: The photographer wanted to take pictures of the terrible

conditions in the factory.

6. The plumber had to get his _____ to fix the pipe.

7. Many _____ come to America for a better life.

8. In an _____ area, there are many factories.

9. The _____ of child labor makes me angry.

10. Failing the test made me

_____.

VOCABULARY **Academic Words** *Use with textbook page 46.*

Read the paragraph below. Pay attention to the underlined academic words.

> Up until the early 1900s, child <u>labor</u> was common in America. Children often worked long hours in dangerous factories. Fortunately, groups like the National Child Labor Committee worked to <u>expose</u> these harsh working conditions. They wanted to improve the <u>welfare</u> of America's poor children. <u>Dramatic</u> photographs of children working in factories and mines made many Americans want to end child labor.

Match each word with its definition.

Example: __*b*__ labor

_____ 1. welfare

_____ 2. expose

_____ 3. dramatic

a. exciting and impressive

b. work, especially work using much physical or mental effort

c. health, comfort, and happiness

d. give people information that was previously hidden

Use the academic words from the exercise above to complete the sentences.

4. I enjoyed the _____ fireworks show.

5. I wanted to _____ the hidden crime.

6. I know that children in the United States used to do hard _____ in factories.

7. Your parents always look out for your _____.

Complete the sentences with your own ideas.

Example: My __*teachers and parents*__ take care of my welfare.

8. I thought _____ was very dramatic.

9. I believe that newspapers should expose the truth _____.

10. I believe child labor is _____.

REMEMBER A *suffix* is a letter or letters added to the end of a word to make a new word. Words that end in *e* follow special rules. If the suffix begins with a consonant, do not drop the *e*, as in *profuse + ly = profusely*. If the suffix begins with a vowel or *y*, drop the *e*, as in *true + ly = truly*. There are some exceptions, such as *awfully*.

Read the words in the box below. Then write each word in the correct column in the chart.

careful	acreage	aching	canoeing	excitement
arguing	hoeing	fiercely	enclosure	sorely

Suffix Begins with a Consonant	Suffix Begins with a Vowel	Exceptions

Create a new word by adding the suffix to each word below. Check a dictionary if needed. Then write the definition next to the new word.

Example: disparage + ment = *disparagement (belittlement, mocking)*

1. illustrate + ive = _____

2. singe + ing = _____

3. nine + th = _____

4. use + age = _____

5. whole + ly = _____

6. expose + ure = _____

7. like + ly = _____

8. virtue + ous = _____

9. marry + age = _____

10. frown + ing = _____

READING STRATEGY **USE VISUALS** *Use with textbook page 47.*

REMEMBER Visuals include photographs, illustrations, cartoons, maps, and graphic organizers. They support the text and provide more information about the topic.

This photograph is from "The Eye of Conscience." Look at it carefully, and answer the questions.

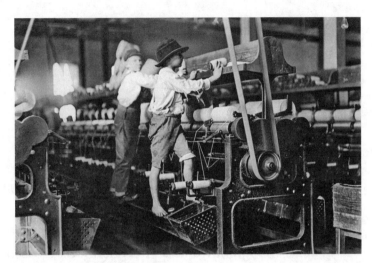

1. What is the photograph of?

   _____

2. When do you think the photograph was taken?

   _____

3. What can you tell about the setting of the photograph?

   _____

   _____

4. What can you tell about the boys in the photograph? Are they rich or poor? How can you tell?

   _____

   _____

5. What information does the photograph give that the text probably could not?

   _____

   _____

Choose the best answer for each item. Circle the letter of the correct answer.

1. In 1909, Lewis Hine began taking pictures of _____.

   a. immigrants   **b.** child performers   **c.** child laborers

2. At the time that Hine began photographing them, the number of child laborers in
   America was _____.

   a. 5,000   **b.** 120,000   **c.** 1.7 million

3. Lewis Hine also took pictures of _____.

   a. celebrities   **b.** royalty   **c.** new immigrants

4. Hine used photography to _____.

   a. advertise products   **b.** fight social injustice   **c.** help big companies

5. One important outcome of Hine's photographs was _____.

   a. bigger profits   **b.** more immigrant workers   **c.** new laws protecting
       for factories   workers

EXTENSION *Use with textbook page 57.*

**Think about a photograph from the article "The Eye of Conscience" that affected
you. Describe it briefly and tell how it made you feel.**

_____

_____

_____

_____

_____

_____

GRAMMAR

Restrictive and Nonrestrictive Relative Clauses *Use with textbook page 58.*

> **REMEMBER** A relative clause describes a noun. A pronoun begins a relative clause. Use the pronouns *who, whom,* and *that* to describe people. Use *that* and *which* to describe things. When a clause is restrictive, it tells us which person, place, or thing the sentence refers to. Nonrestrictive clauses give extra information, but the sentence is clear without them. Use commas with nonrestrictive clauses.

Read each sentence. Write whether it has a restrictive or nonrestrictive relative clause.

Example: Ali is the boy whose bike I borrowed. _____*restrictive*_____

1. My mother is the artist who made this beautiful painting. _____

2. I rode the bike, which is green, all the way to town. _____

3. George was late again, which means his mother will be angry. _____

4. I met the explorer who made it all the way to the North Pole. _____

5. Mrs. Henderson, who used to be my teacher, lives in Florida. _____

Complete each of the sentences below with a restrictive or nonrestrictive relative clause.

Example: (that) I want the digital camera _____*that has the best lens*_____.

6. (who) A good teacher, _____.

7. (whose) I am the person _____.

8. (which) I want to live in Los Angeles, _____.

9. (who) I know a lot of people _____.

10. (that) I know a shop _____.

Describe an Experience *Use with textbook page 59.*

This is the graphic organizer that Santos completed before writing his paragraph.

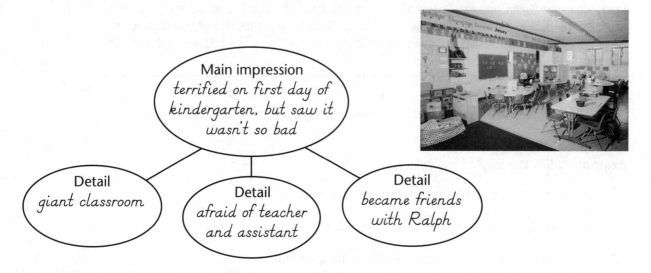

Main impression
terrified on first day of kindergarten, but saw it wasn't so bad

Detail
giant classroom

Detail
afraid of teacher and assistant

Detail
became friends with Ralph

Complete your own graphic organizer about an important event or experience in your life.

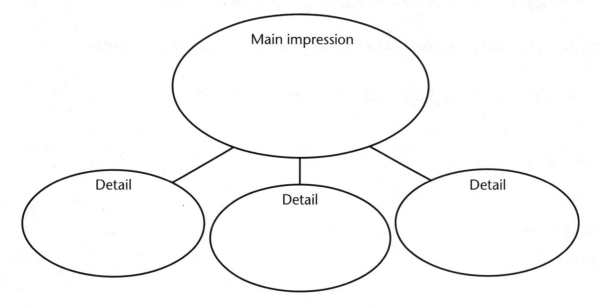

Main impression

Detail

Detail

Detail

Name _____ Date _____

What is light?

READING 5: "Visiting the Edison Museum"

TEXT ANALYSIS **Analyzing Procedural Texts**
Use with textbook pages 61–62.

> **REMEMBER** **Procedural texts** tell you how to do something. They describe a process. Procedural texts include instructions and directions.

Read the following excerpt from a procedural text and fill out the chart below it.

> **Troubleshooting**: If your TV remote control unit does not operate, one of the following may be the problem.
> a. Is the FUNCTION switch set correctly?
> b. Are the batteries inserted with polarity aligned?
> c. Are the batteries worn out?
> d. Are you using it under strong lighting?
> e. Is anything blocking the remote control sensor on the TV set?

Circle the X next to the sentence that would make each step in the procedure easier for the reader to understand.

a	X X	Slide the switch to the TV position. The switch must be in the right position.
b	X X	Polarity refers to the positive and negative ends of the battery. The end of the battery marked + must match the end of the battery holder marked +.
c	X X	Another name for battery is voltaic cell. Try replacing them with new batteries.
d	X X	Strong light can interfere with the remote, so try dimming the lights. Strong light can interfere with the remote, the way a loud noise can make it hard to hear someone whispering.
e	X X	The remote control sensor receives the light signal from the remote control unit. The remote control sensor is on the lower-right corner of the front of the TV set.

> **REMEMBER** Paying attention to how a text is organized can help you understand what you read. Some common **organizational patterns** are cause and effect, classification, and problem-solution. Noticing the organizational pattern can help you **make inferences**, or "educated guesses" about unstated but implied information.

Read the excerpt below about house flies. Then answer the questions.

From "The House Fly and How to Suppress It" by L.O. Howard and F.C. Bishopp (1925)

[I]t is often necessary to catch or otherwise destroy adult flies, or to protect food materials from contamination and persons from annoyance or danger. . . .

Flytraps may be used to advantage in decreasing the number of flies. Their use has been advocated not only because of the immediate results, but because of the chances that the flies may be caught before they lay eggs, and the number of future generations will be reduced greatly.

The effectiveness of the traps will depend on the selection of baits. A good bait for catching house flies is 1 part of blackstrap molasses to 3 parts of water, after the mixture has been allowed to ferment for a day or two. . . . A mixture of equal parts brown sugar and curd of sour milk, thoroughly moistened, gives good results [also].

What organizational pattern does this passage use? Circle the correct answer.

problem-solution   chronological   cause and effect

Underline each statement that is a reasonable inference based on the passage.

1. Flies are attracted to wet, sugary foods.

2. There's little point in preventing flies from laying eggs; using flytraps is preferred.

3. The common house fly is different from other types of flies.

4. There are no other methods of preventing house flies.

TEXT ANALYSIS

> **REMEMBER** Being aware of a text's organizational pattern can help you draw complex conclusions about what you read. A conclusion is an idea that you can get from thinking a step beyond what the text says. This means you make a judgment based on the information a text provides.

Read the excerpt below about conversations. Then answer the question.

From Conversation: What to Say and How to Say It
by Mary Greer Conklin (1912)

The aim and design of conversation is, therefore, pleasure. . . . Conversation, above all, is dialogue, not monologue. It is a partnership, not an individual affair. . . . Monopolizing tyrants of society who will allow no dog to bark in their presence are not conversationalists; they are lecturers. . . . The good conversationalists are not the ones who dominate the talk in any gathering. They are the people who have the grace to contribute something of their own while generously drawing out the best that is in others.

What organizational pattern does the paragraph use? Circle the correct answer.

problem-solution   contrast   cause and effect

Based on this excerpt, draw a conclusion about what Mary Greer Conklin thought about listening skills.

_____

_____

_____

_____

REMEMBER Graphic sources, such as charts and graphs, provide information visually. To understand a graphic source, you may need to examine the title and the labels. When you analyze multiple graphic sources, you will need to determine what the sources have in common and how they differ.

The chart below shows the specifications for four personal music players. Use the chart to answer the questions below the chart.

	Scooter	Peerless	SuperSolid	FullScreen
Consumer rating	★	★★★★★	★★★★★	★★★
Capacity (songs)	500	4,000	30,000	7,000
Price	$69	$199	$249	$399
Battery life	12 hours	24 hours	36 hours	36 hours
Wireless capability	None	None	None	Wi-Fi
Screen size	No screen	2-inch	2.5-inch	3.5-inch
Warranty	None	None	Limited (3 months)	Extended (2 years)

1. Which music player holds the most songs? _____

2. Which music players cost less than $200? _____

3. What factors seem to contribute to a high consumer rating? (Circle answers.)

   high song capacity   low cost   large screen size

4. If you were considering buying a personal music player, which one would you choose? Which one seems to be the best value? Explain your answer.

   _____

   _____

   _____

   _____

TEXT ANALYSIS **Analyzing Data in Graphic Sources**
Use with textbook page 64.

Look at the chart below. Remember to read the title and all additional information. Then answer the questions below.

Languages Spoken at Home in the United States

	Population*	English only	Asian and Pacific languages	Indo-European languages	Spanish
Austin, TX	731,000	489,000	24,000	22,000	191,000
Boston, MA	609,000	405,000	35,000	69,000	90,000
Chicago, IL	2,639,000	1,734,000	93,000	164,000	614,000
Los Angeles, CA	3,546,000	1,399,000	301,000	236,000	1,555,000
Seattle, WA	582,000	461,000	59,000	24,000	26,000

* aged five years and over   Source: *U.S. Census Bureau*

1. Of the two cities with the highest population, which has a greater number of

   residents who speak only English in the home? _____

2. Compare the data for Austin and Seattle. Which city has the greater number of

   residents who speak Indo-European languages at home? _____

3. Which city has the fewest residents who speak Asian and Pacific Island languages at

   home? _____

4. Why do you think the U.S. Census counted only people who were five years old and

   above? _____

Examine Figures 5 and 6 in Unit 1. Then answer the question below.

5. What is the difference between Figure 5 and Figure 6? What do they each show?

   _____

   _____

   _____

TEXT ANALYSIS **Summarizing and Critiquing Text** *Use with textbook page 66.*

> **REMEMBER** When you **summarize** a text, you tell the main idea and the most important elements of the text, without adding your opinion. When you **critique** a text, you evaluate the information the author presents and the way he or she presents it. You form an opinion.

Read the following two paragraphs. Then answer the questions below.

> **A.** Beverly Gherman's book *Ansel Adams: America's Photographer* is a biography that covers Ansel Adams's life. In addition to Adams's childhood in California and his family life, she describes the influence of nature on his life and his photography. Adams's various photographic methods are also covered.
>
> **B.** Beverly Gherman's book *Ansel Adams: America's Photographer* provides an interesting and insightful glimpse into Adams's life. One of the biography's greatest strengths is the way Gherman describes important events in Adams's life, some of which influenced his art. For example, she describes how Adams's nose was once broken during an earthquake. Such details help us understand his sense of awe toward the natural world.

1. Which paragraph is a summary? Which is a critique? Explain your answer.

   _____

   _____

2. Choose a book or story you remember well. On the lines below, write two short paragraphs. The first paragraph should be a summary, and the second paragraph should be a critique.

   _____

   _____

   _____

   _____

   _____

   _____

WRITING

Write a Procedural Document *Use with textbook page 72.*

Use this flowchart to help you think through the prewriting stage of your procedural document.

What is my topic?
(Be sure it is not too large or complicated. You may need to choose just one part of it.)

Do I need to research it? If so, where?
(Some topics can be researched on the Internet. Others will require library research.)

Who are my readers and how much do they know?
(This will help you decide how to start and whether you can skip some steps.)

WRITING

Edit and Proofread *Use with textbook page 75.*

Read the draft of an e-mail letter below. Look for mistakes in spelling, punctuation, and grammar. Mark your corrections between the lines.

To the members of the Computer Club:
We will be having a special speeker for our next meeting. Wouldn't it would be great to
have a good turnout for her. Here's the information:
Speaker's bio
Jackie Demas is a video game programer with ten year's experience in the feild. She
now has her own business Demas and Associates. She has been speeking about
careers in the programming field for five years' and is considered an entertaining and
informative speaker.
Meeting time and place
The meeting will be in Room 143 at 3:00 on wednesday, march 3.
Refreshments
Jaime is in charge of the sandwiches and Paolo is bringing the juice. Gina will bring a
fruit and vegetable platter for people.
I hope to see you all there,
Karen

EDIT AND PROOFREAD   *Use with textbook page 82.*

Read the paragraph carefully. Look for mistakes in spelling, punctuation, and grammar. Correct the mistakes with the editing marks on Student Book page 553. Then rewrite the paragraph correctly on the lines below.

> I am glad I live at Los Angeles. Our family went on a bike ride on the park this week end. We rode to the park near our house. the park is in the other end of our street. I rode my red new bike who I got for my birthday. I raced my brother who is seventeen years old. He won, but it was Fun anyway. I always like rideing. I saw a friend who's house is nearby. We all had a picnic, when we got to the park. We ate bagles cheese and fresh apples. My friend and I went fishing in the lake. We caught a big fish!

_____

_____

_____

_____

_____

_____

_____

_____

_____

_____

Underline the vocabulary items you know and can use well. Review and practice any you haven't underlined. Underline them when you know them well.

Literary Words	Key Words		Academic Words	
onomatopoeia	concave	conditions	author	approached
repetition	convex	equipment	culture	despite
irony	opaque	immigrants	text	equivalent
imagery	translucent	industrial	tradition	visual
setting	transparent	inhumanity	energy	dramatic
	wavelength	miserable	interpret	expose
			transmit	labor
			virtual	welfare
			visible	

Put a check by the skills you can perform well. Review and practice any you haven't checked off. Check them off when you can perform them well.

Skills	I can . . .
Word Study	☐ recognize and use compound words. ☐ recognize and spell words with *-le* and *-el*. ☐ identify and use antonyms. ☐ recognize and spell suffixes.
Reading Strategies	☐ predict. ☐ skim. ☐ visualize. ☐ use visuals.
Grammar	☐ use correct adjective order. ☐ use adverb clauses of time. ☐ use prepositions of place. ☐ use restrictive and nonrestrictive relative clauses.
Writing	☐ describe a character. ☐ describe an object. ☐ describe a place. ☐ describe an experience. ☐ write a procedural document. ☐ write a descriptive essay.

Visual Literacy: Smithsonian American
Art Museum *Use with textbook pages 84–85.*

LEARNING TO LOOK

Look at *Sun* by Arthur Dove on page 85 in your textbook. Place a blank piece of
paper over the top half of the painting so you cannot see the sun. Write three
observations about what you see in the bottom half of the painting. State facts,
not opinions.

Observations for Bottom Half of *Sun*

Example: *There is a yellow circle with a blue center.* _____

1. _____

2. _____

3. _____

Cover the bottom half of *Sun* with a blank piece of paper. Write three observations
about what you see in the top half of the painting.

Observations for Top Half of *Sun*

Example: *There is a black circle.* _____

1. _____

2. _____

3. _____

INTERPRETATION

Look at *Sun* again and *Plate #753* by Robert Sperry on page 85 in your textbook. Both artists use circles to show usually unseen forces such as gravity at work in the universe.

1. Imagine that you had to create a work of art that represents daytime sky. What shape would you use to represent the sun? Why did you choose that shape?

   _____

   _____

2. Now select a different shape that could represent the sun. Why did you choose that shape?

   _____

   _____

5W&H

Look at *Ryder's House* by Edward Hopper on page 84 in your textbook. Imagine that you had to knock on the door of that house and interview whoever answers. Write down six questions that you would ask them, using Who, Where, When, What, Why, and How to guide you.

Example: Who _was Ryder?_____

1. Who _____

2. Where _____

3. When _____

4. What _____

5. Why _____

6. How _____

How are growth and change related?

READING 1: "How Seeds and Plants Grow" /
"Two Brothers and the Pumpkin Seeds"

VOCABULARY **Key Words** *Use with textbook page 89.*

Write each word in the box next to its definition.

develop	embryo	germination	inactive	protective	straighten

Example: _germination_ : the process in which a seed starts to grow

1. _____: used to keep something safe from harm

2. _____: become or make straight

3. _____: grow or change into something bigger or more advanced

4. _____: not doing anything; not active

5. _____: a tiny young plant contained within the seed

Use the words in the box at the top of the page to complete the sentences.

6. Many animals and plants have a _____ covering, such as a shell.

7. A plant _____ is the plant in its earliest stage of development.

8. Plants can only _____ when they have the right amount of light, water, and food.

9. Until a seed begins to germinate, we say it is _____.

10. Many plants are curved when they first sprout, but they _____ as they grow.

Read the paragraph. Pay attention to the underlined academic words.

> The saguaro cactus is a very tough plant. It is able to survive in the hot, dry environment of deserts in Arizona and Mexico. The saguaro has sharp spines, which function as a form of protection. They keep potential predators from eating the plant. The saguaro cactus can live up to 250 years, but its growth process is very slow.

Write academic words from the paragraph next to their correct definitions.

Example: *environment* : the land, water, and air in which plants live

1. _____ : a series of actions, developments, or changes that happen in a sequence

2. _____ : possible

3. _____ : the usual purpose of a thing

Use academic words from the paragraph to complete the sentences.

4. Plants that grow in a dry _____ must be able to live without much water.

5. The _____ of the seed coat is to protect the plant.

6. All seeds contain _____ plants, but some of them never develop into actual plants.

7. Different kinds of plants follow the exact same _____ for growth.

Complete the sentences with your own ideas.

Example: In the process of germination, a seed *begins to grow into a plant* .

8. The function of the seed coat is _____ .

9. The environment a plant grows in can be _____ .

10. Each seed has a potential _____ inside it.

WORD STUDY Related Words *Use with textbook page 91.*

REMEMBER Related words are words that are in the same word family, they share the same base word, and have related meanings. There are similarities and differences between the words. Knowing the meaning of the base word can help you figure out the meaning of other words in that family.
Example: transport (verb) = move or carry goods or people from place to place
  transportation (noun) = the process of transporting
  transported (adjective) = taken or carried from place to place

Look at the words in the first column of the chart. Write a related noun and adjective for each word.

Verb	Noun	Adjective
improve	*improvement*	*improved*
1. pollute		
2. develop		
3. relate		
4. correct		
5. combine		
6. amaze		

Look at the words in the chart below. Write a related word. Then write a sentence using the related word.

Word	Related Word	Sentence
fascinate	*fascination*	*He had a fascination with plants.*
7. inspire		
8. communicate		
9. alternate		
10. conceal		
11. add		
12. compose		
13. refresh		
14. infect		
15. amend		

REMEMBER To recognize sequence, look for key words as you read, such as *first, then, next, finally,* and *after.* Keep track of events by listing them in order, or make a chart showing the steps.

Read the paragraph and underline the words that indicate sequence.

The life cycle of a plant begins with a seed. First, the seed coat swells and breaks open. Next, a tiny root grows down into the soil. Then a stem grows up toward the surface of the soil. Later, leaves form on the stem. Finally, the plant forms more seeds, and the life cycle begins again.

Read the passage. Then answer the questions.

After school, the phone rang. It was my friend Julia. She said, "I forgot my house key. Can I come over to your house and wait there till my Mom can come for me?"

I said, "Sure." Then the phone rang again. This time, it was my friend Alfred. He said, "My Dad has to go to a meeting. Can I do my homework at your house?"

I said, "No problem." While I was hanging up the phone, the doorbell rang. Both Julia and Alfred were standing there. "That was quick!" I laughed.

Later, my Dad came home. "What are all these kids doing here?" he asked.

Finally, both Julia's mom and Alfred's dad came to pick them up. After they left, I got ready for bed and went to sleep.

1. What was the first thing that happened in the story?

   _____

2. What happened while the narrator was hanging up the phone after speaking with Alfred?

   _____

3. What happened next?

   _____

4. Who picked up Julia and Alfred?

   _____

5. What did the narrator do before going to sleep?

   _____

COMPREHENSION *Use with textbook page 96.*

Choose the best answer for each item. Circle the letter of the correct answer.

1. A seed has three important parts, which are _____.

   a. the stem, roots and leaves

   b. the embryo, stored food, and seed coat

   c. the plastic wrap, roots and embryo

2. The time when an embryo first begins to grow is called _____.

   a. photosynthesis

   b. germination

   c. protection

3. Photosynthesis happens when _____.

   a. a plant has no seed coat

   b. a plant fails to germinate

   c. a plant makes its own food

4. The swallow rewarded Kim's generosity with _____.

   a. a lotus blossom

   b. a pumpkin seed

   c. a worm

5. Chang was punished for being _____.

   a. cruel and greedy

   b. full of pride

   c. afraid of birds

EXTENSION *Use with textbook page 97.*

Some plants go through the whole life cycle in one year, starting as seeds and dying when they have produced new seeds. They are called annual plants. (*Annual* means "yearly.") Some plants keep growing and getting bigger for years. They may die back at the end of the season, but they sprout up again in the spring. They are called perennial plants. (*Perennial* means "living more than one year.") Write the names of four kinds of plants in the chart below. Then research the plant in order to find out if it is an annual or a perennial plant. Complete the chart.

Plant	Type
morning glory	annual

Sequence Words *Use with textbook page 98.*

> **REMEMBER** Sequence words show the order of events. Frequently used sequence words and phrases
> include *first, then, next, after that, afterwards, following that, last,* and *finally. Then, next, after that,* and
> *following that* all mean the same thing. Use a comma after all sequence words except for *then.*

**The following sentences present events in the order in which they happened.
Insert a sequence word or phrase from the box to show the order of the events.**

| Finally, | Next, | Following that, | First, | Then |

1. _____ she awoke.

2. _____ she got dressed.

3. _____ she went to the kitchen.

4. _____ she ate breakfast.

5. _____ she left for school.

**The following sentences present a series of events in the wrong order. Write *first,
next, afterwards, following that,* and *last* to show the correct order.**

6. _____ go to the store and buy the ingredients you do
not have.

7. _____ put the mixture in a pan and put it in the oven.

8. _____ decide what kind of cake you want to make.

9. _____ mix the ingredients together.

10. _____ check that you have all the ingredients.

WRITING

Write a Story with a Starter *Use with textbook page 99.*

This is the sequence-of-events chart that Nicholas completed before writing his paragraph.

> **First,**
> *The plant wrapped around me and I cut my way out.*

↓

> **Then**
> *A park ranger told me not to touch the plant because it was rare.*

↓

> **Finally,**
> *The plant was still in perfect condition. Had it been a daydream?*

Complete your own sequence-of-events chart using a story starter.

> **First,**

↓

> **Then**

↓

> **Finally,**

How are growth and change related?

READING 2: From *Roll of Thunder, Hear My Cry*

VOCABULARY   **Literary Words** *Use with textbook page 101.*

REMEMBER The **point of view** is the angle a story is told from. In a first-person point of view, the narrator uses the pronoun *I*. In a third-person point of view, the narrator uses the pronouns *he, she*. The **plot** is the sequence of connected events that make up the story. They can be presented in a logical order that is linear or in a mixed-up order that is nonlinear. The **conflict** is the struggle between two opposing forces that sets the plot in motion.

Read the paragraph. Then answer the questions.

> Alia ran into the room, her eyes shining. She exclaimed, "I won the art competition! They have offered me a scholarship. I will be able to go to art school next year!"
>
> Her parents frowned. They wanted her to go to business school. They wanted her to be a bookkeeper, maybe even an accountant. These were reliable, well-paying jobs.
>
> Before her parents could say a word, Alia continued. "Here, look at the information my art teacher gave me. There are a lot of good jobs for people with an art degree. Studying art does not mean I will never have a steady job."
>
> Alia's parents took the pages she was holding and began to read. After a few minutes, her father looked up and smiled. "Yes, Alia," he said. "I can see that studying art will give you a lot of options. Since you want this so much, I think your mother and I will have to agree."
>
> Alia ran forward and threw her arms around her mother and father. "Thank you!" she cried.

1. Whose point of view is the story written in? _____

2. What is the conflict in the story? How does it get resolved?

   _____

3. Summarize the plot in one sentence. _____

4. Imagine the story was told from Alia's perspective, in the first-person point of view. Write the first two sentences in the first-person point of view.

   _____

VOCABULARY **Academic Words** *Use with textbook page 102.*

Read the paragraph. Pay attention to the underlined academic words.

> I saw a movie about a teenage girl who faced <u>discrimination</u> when she tried out for a boys' high school soccer team. Before trying out for the team, she was very excited and filled with <u>anticipation</u>. During the tryout, some of the boys laughed and teased her. She was hurt by their <u>reaction</u>, but she didn't let it <u>affect</u> her playing. She had to work hard, but she finally made it on the team.

Match each word with its definition.

Example: ___*b*___ affect

a. a feeling of excitement because something good or fun is going to happen

_____ **1.** reaction

b. cause a person to feel strong emotions

_____ **2.** anticipation

c. the practice of treating one group of people differently from another in an unfair way

_____ **3.** discrimination

d. something you say or do because of what has happened or been said to you

Use the academic words from the exercise above to complete the sentences.

4. The Civil Rights Movement of the 1960s worked to end _____.

5. I was filled with _____ as I waited for my sister at the airport.

6. When everyone yelled "Happy Birthday!" I had a surprised _____.

7. My decision will _____ the whole family.

Complete the sentences with your own ideas.

Example: His reaction to the funny movie ___*made me laugh too*___.

8. The anticipation of the holidays _____.

9. Discrimination is wrong because _____.

10. I didn't let _____ affect my concentration.

REMEMBER Homographs are two or more words that have the same spelling but different meanings.
Example: Can we *address* this issue later? *versus* What is your *address*?
Homographs are not always pronounced the same. Often homographs are different parts of speech.
The context will help you decide which meaning is appropriate.

Read each sentence and circle the meaning of the underlined homograph.

Example: The famous actor gave his autograph to a <u>fan</u>. ((a follower) / a cooling device)

1. It is so hot today, I need to turn on the <u>fan</u>. (a follower / a cooling device)

2. I'll just open a <u>can</u> of tuna for dinner tonight. (to be able to / container)

3. Please don't <u>tear</u> my shirt. It's all new! (liquid from one's eyes / to break)

4. This party is fun. I am having a <u>ball</u>! (sports equipment / great fun)

5. The students this year are exceptionally <u>bright</u>. (light / intelligent)

Read the definitions in the box. Choose the two definitions that go with the homographs, and write them in the chart.

secure	child	part of the alphabet	solid
~~to annoy~~	to care for	similar	
to offer	container for valuables	written communication	
to joke	gift	~~insect~~	

Homograph	1st definition	2nd definition
bug	*insect*	*to annoy*
6. kid		
7. letter		
8. like		
9. present		
10. safe		

Name _____ Date _____

READING STRATEGY | COMPARE AND CONTRAST

Use with textbook page 103.

> **REMEMBER** When you **compare**, you see how things are similar. When you **contrast**, you see how things are different.

Read each paragraph and answer the questions about how the characters feel.

> Kevin sat at the end of the dock and dipped his toe into the water. It was freezing. Kevin turned when he heard his sister's voice. Lily was smiling.
>
> "Oh, the water looks great," she cried. "I can't wait to jump in and cool off!"
>
> Lily dove right in and shouted to Kevin, "Come on in! The water is great!"
>
> "It is freezing!" Kevin said. "I think I am going to wait right here." Even though he really wanted to swim, the cold water was just too cold for him.

1. **Compare** the way Kevin and Lily feel. How do they feel alike?

   _____

2. **Contrast** the way Kevin and Lily feel. How do they feel different?

   _____

> Nola and Terry looked at the yard in shock. They had agreed to mow Mrs. Power's lawn, but they hadn't expected this. The grass hadn't been cut in weeks.
>
> Terry said, "There's no way we'll ever get it all done. And it's so hot!"
>
> "I know how you feel," said Nola, "but Mrs. Powers is counting on us. Until her ankle is better, she really can't do the work herself. She's always been so nice to us. I feel we should do something for her in return."

3. **Compare** the way Nola and Terry feel. How do they feel alike?

   _____

4. **Contrast** the way Nola and Terry feel. How do they feel different?

   _____

5. How does the skill of comparing and contrasting help you to understand a story better?

   _____

Choose the best answer for each item. Circle the letter of the correct answer.

1. Cassie is excited when her teacher tells her that they are getting new books because

   _____.

   a. she finds class boring and thinks the books will be interesting
   b. her little sister loves to read books
   c. she has never had a book of her own

2. Cassie feels sinking disappointment when she sees that _____.

   a. the books are old and dirty
   b. Mrs. Crocker won't give her a book
   c. Little Man doesn't want to read

3. Little Man throws his book on the floor when he sees _____.

   a. that it has stories he has read many times before
   b. Mrs. Crocker staring at him
   c. that the book has been given to students by race

4. Mrs. Crocker calls Little Man to the front of the room to _____.

   a. whip him
   b. send him home
   c. give him a new book

5. At the end, Cassie tells Mrs. Crocker _____.

   a. that she is leaving school
   b. that she doesn't want her book either
   c. that she has no right to treat Little Man badly

RESPONSE TO LITERATURE *Use with textbook page 111.*

In this excerpt, connected events make up the plot of the story. Fill in the graphic organizer with four of these connected events.

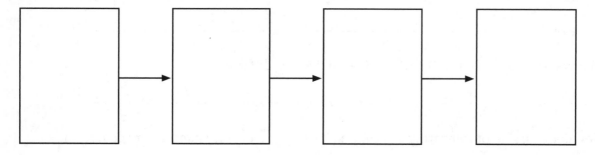

GRAMMAR

Conditional Sentences *Use with textbook page 112.*

> **REMEMBER** The factual conditional describes the future and often uses *will* in the result clause. The unreal conditional describes something that is contrary to fact. It uses the simple past in the *if* clause and *could, would,* or *might* + the base form of a verb in the result clause. If the verb in the *if* clause is *be,* use *were* for all persons.

Write *F* on the line if the sentence contains a factual conditional statement. Write *U* if the sentence contains an unreal conditional statement.

_____ 1. If she were rich, she might travel all over the world.

_____ 2. We will win this game if he hits a home run.

Complete the sentences below. Follow the directions in parentheses, and write the verbs in the correct tense or form.

Example: (Use *work* and *be* to express the unreal conditional.) He

____*would work*_____ outside most of the time if he

_____*were*_____ a farmer.

3. (Use *cancel* and *rain* to express the factual conditional.) The

coaches _____ the game if it

_____.

4. (Use *invade* and *try* to express the unreal conditional.) If aliens from

another planet _____ Earth, our teacher

_____ to teach them English.

5. (Use *win* and *complete* to express the factual conditional.) If we

_____ the city baseball championship, we

_____ for the state title.

Rewrite a Familiar Story *Use with textbook page 113.*

This is the T-chart that Leah completed before writing her paragraph.

Cassie's Point of View	Little Man's Point of View
I knew Little Man would be disappointed when he saw the dirty books. Little Man started jumping on his book. Miss Crocker was going to switch him! I looked inside the book and saw why Little Man was so furious.	The book was so old and dirty that I didn't want to touch it. A chart in the book had awful words. I stomped hard to make the words go away. I refused to pick up the book even if it meant the switch.

Complete your own T-chart about a familiar story from a new point of view.

Familiar Point of View	New Point of View

How are growth and change related?

READING 3: "Migration Patterns"

VOCABULARY **Key Words** *Use with textbook page 115.*

Write each word in the box next to its definition.

declined	property	residents	rural	trend	urban

Example: _____*declined*_____ : decreased in value or amount

1. _____ : the way a situation is changing or developing

2. _____ : people who live in a particular place

3. _____ : something that is owned, such as land

4. _____ : located in the countryside or related to country life

5. _____ : located in a city or related to city life

Use the words in the box at the top of the page to complete the sentences.

6. In my hometown, people have moved away and the population has steadily

    _____ .

7. My landlord has sold some of his _____ to raise money.

8. When the United States first became a nation, most people lived far from the cities

    in _____ areas.

9. I live in an _____
    area, where there are lots of
    museums, theaters, and people.

10. Because I live in a small town,

    most of the _____
    know each other.

Read the paragraph below. Pay attention to the underlined academic words.

In the United States during the early 1900s, the population <u>distribution</u> changed greatly. Many African Americans moved from southern rural areas to northern cities. This <u>migration</u> was caused by several <u>factors</u>. One important factor was the large number of factory jobs in the north. African Americans from the southern <u>region</u> moved to cities like New York and Chicago to get better paying jobs. By 1930, the African American population in the North had risen by 20 <u>percent</u>.

Write academic words from the paragraph above next to their correct definitions.

Example: _____*percent*_____: equal to a particular amount in every hundred

1. _____: fairly large area of a state or country, usually without exact limits

2. _____: things that influence or cause a situation

3. _____: scattering or spreading of something over an area

4. _____: action of a large group of animals, including people, moving from one place to another

Use academic words from the paragraph above to complete the sentences.

5. There is a severe storm watch for the entire _____ tonight.

6. At least 90 _____ of the money my school raised was used to help the neighborhood.

7. Every year I watch the butterfly _____ as they fly south for the winter.

8. The _____ of schools and hospitals influences where people buy houses.

Complete the sentences with your own ideas.

Example: Some factors that influence my decisions are
_____*my friends' opinions and my interests*_____.

9. Migrations happen because _____.

10. The region where I live is _____.

Name _____ Date _____

WORD STUDY Long *a, i, o* Spelling Patterns

Use with textbook page 117.

> **REMEMBER** The long vowel sounds can be spelled several different ways. Long *a* can be spelled *a_e* as in *make*, *ai* as in *maid*, and *ay* as in *day*. Long *i* can be spelled *i_e* as in *mile* and *igh* as in *night*. Long *o* can be spelled *o_e* as in *stone* and *ow* as in *mow*.

Read the words in the box. Then write each word in the correct column in the chart.

~~shape~~	flight	below	promote	slime	hay
bow	grape	afraid	mime	might	remote

Long *a*	Long *i*	Long *o*
a_e	*i_e*	*o_e*
shape		

Long *a*	Long *i*	Long *o*
ai, ay	*igh*	*ow*

Look at each row of words. Circle the word in each row that contains the long vowel sound in parentheses.

1. (long *a*)   hassle   betray   clap

2. (long *o*)   shop   mope   plot

3. (long *i*)   life   little   list

4. (long *a*)   flat   maid   battle

5. (long *o*)   grow   lost   lobster

REMEMBER When you **scan** something, look for particular things that you want to know. Look at the title, visuals, and move your eyes quickly over the words. Stop scanning and begin reading when you see the key words you need.

Scan the paragraphs below. Look for information about what Jacinda has done over her summer break. List three things she did below.

I was really excited to go back to school. I missed all my friends and my favorite teachers. I had a great summer though. We spent July in a cabin near a lake in New York. My family goes there every year. I spent the days swimming, and seeing other kids my age who also spend their summers there. My favorite part was at night because my parents would grill food and we'd eat outdoors at a picnic table and look at the stars.

In August we came back home. I started taking tennis lessons at the nearby YMCA. I'm a good player but I want to be even better. Me and my friend Denise played just about every day.

A week before school started we went to visit my Grandmother in North Carolina. I hadn't seen her since last Christmas so it was great to spend some time with her again. She's a photographer. We hung out in her darkroom and I helped her develop photographs. It was a lot of fun!

1. _____

2. _____

3. _____

4. Scan the above paragraphs. Write what was Jacinda's favorite part about her month at the lake in New York.

   _____

   _____

5. Scan the above paragraphs. What did Jacinda do with her grandmother. Write your answer below.

   _____

   _____

COMPREHENSION *Use with textbook page 122.*

Choose the best answer for each item. Circle the letter of the correct answer.

1. In 2002 to 2003, most moves were _____.

   a. overseas   **b.** to another state   **c.** within the same county

2. The people who move least often are _____.

   a. widowed people   **b.** single people   **c.** married people

3. Compared to people who own their homes, people who rent move _____.

   a. more often   **b.** less often   **c.** at about the same rate

4. If today's trend of moving to different regions continues, more people in the future may move to the _____.

   a. Midwest   **b.** South   **c.** Northeast

5. If more people move to the South, the Northeast may become _____.

   a. more crowded   **b.** more rural   **c.** less populated

EXTENSION *Use with textbook page 123.*

The article on migration patterns names four regions of the United States. There is also a fifth region, the Pacific region. Research to find out which states are part of each region. Then write at least one state name for each region in the chart.

Region	State
Northeast	
South	
West	
Midwest	
Pacific	

Simple Past and Present Perfect *Use with textbook page 124.*

> **REMEMBER** Use the simple past to show that an action began and ended at a definite point in the past. Use the present perfect to show that an action began in the past and ended at an unspecified time or continues into the present.

Write *SP* on the line if the sentence is in the simple past. Write *PP* if the sentence is in the present perfect.

_____ 1. The United States first conducted a census in 1790.

_____ 2. The U.S. population has become more diverse recently.

_____ 3. Last year Nevada grew faster than any other state.

_____ 4. Lately, Arizona has grown faster than Nevada.

_____ 5. The population of Louisiana decreased after Hurricane Katrina.

Complete the following sentences with the correct form of the verb in parentheses. Depending on the context of the sentence, use either the simple past or the present perfect.

Example: (shrink) The population of Europe ___*has shrunk*___ in recent years.

6. (use) In 1890, census takers first _____ data-processing machines.

7. (be) For many centuries, California _____ a popular destination for immigrants.

8. (move) In recent years, more people _____ to the United States from Mexico than from any other country.

9. (establish) The government _____ the Census Bureau in 1902.

10. (play) Ever since then, the Census Bureau _____ an important role in the study of the U.S. population.

Name _____ Date _____

WRITING

Write a Personal Letter *Use with textbook page 125.*

This is the word web that Adrian completed before writing his paragraph.

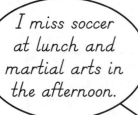

I miss soccer at lunch and martial arts in the afternoon.

I met a kid named Ricardo who also likes soccer.

Me
Adrian

I had to give away my dog.

I think Ricardo and I are going to try out for the soccer team.

Complete your own word web for a personal letter to a friend or family member.

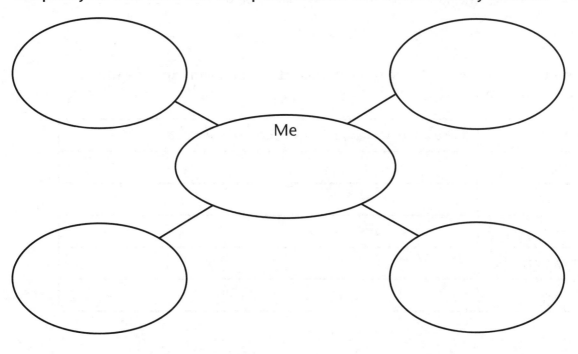

Me

Unit 2 • Reading 3

61

VOCABULARY **Literary Words** *Use with textbook page 127.*

REMEMBER Writers use **characterization** to show what a character is like by describing what the character thinks and does. One way to show that is through **dialogue**—conversations between characters. Dialogue always appears in quotation marks. **Sarcasm** is a form of speech that expresses criticism or annoyance sometimes with humor. It often means the opposite of what is said.

Label each sentence with the literary word it refers to.

Example: I called Jenna and asked, "Do you want to come over and hang out?"

_____*dialogue*_____

1. This is great weather, it has rained for five days straight. _____

2. I did well on the quiz even though I was very nervous. _____

3. Jeremy and Ida both enjoy going to the movies. _____

4. Ty looked at his friend and said, "I thought we agreed on this." _____

5. I just love taking tests, it's my favorite thing to do. _____

Write sentences that use dialogue to show characterization and express each emotion in the chart.

anger	*"I can't believe you just did that!" she shouted.*
6. sadness	
7. happiness	
8. surprise	
9. nervousness	
10. curiosity	

VOCABULARY **Academic Words** *Use with textbook page 128.*

Read the paragraph. Pay attention to the underlined academic words.

> I was shopping with my little brother when he saw an expensive toy he wanted. I told him we didn't have enough money for it, and he began crying and screaming. At first, I tried to <u>ignore</u> him. My brother's <u>conduct</u>, though, was making other shoppers turn to look. I tried to firmly <u>instruct</u> him to be quiet. I told him that if he didn't stop crying, we would have to leave. With <u>reluctance</u>, my brother finally quieted down and I was very relieved.

Match each word with its definition.

Example: ___c___ reluctance

_____ **1.** ignore

_____ **2.** instruct

_____ **3.** conduct

a. pay no attention to someone or something

b. officially tell someone what to do or how to do something

c. unwillingness to do something

d. the way someone behaves

Use the academic words from the exercise above to complete the sentences.

4. When she gets angry, she will _____ people until she gets over it, acting as if they are not even there.

5. I cannot do what you _____ me to do.

6. To avoid detention, we promised to have better _____ in the future.

7. With _____, I lent my friend my weekly allowance.

Complete the sentences with your own ideas.

Example: Don't ignore ___*signs of the flu or you'll end up*___ feeling worse.

8. My best friend's conduct was _____.

9. People can sometimes overcome their reluctance to _____

_____.

10. Before you start to _____ you should have someone instruct you how to do it.

> **REMEMBER** An idiom is a group of words with a special meaning. Sometimes you can figure out the meaning from context. Other times, you may need to use a dictionary.

Read the sentences. Think about the meaning of each underlined idiom. Next to each sentence, write the letter of the correct definition for each idiom from the chart below. Use a dictionary if needed.

1. _____ When her dog ran away, <u>she went to pieces</u>.

2. _____ You should <u>come clean</u> and tell your friend that you lost her sweater.

3. _____ We were <u>at a loss for words</u> and just stood there silently.

4. _____ Something is not right, but I can't <u>put my finger on it</u>.

5. _____ The test was <u>a piece of cake</u> and he got all the answers right.

6. _____ I'd like to help you out, but my <u>hands are tied</u>.

Definitions	
a. be very easy	d. be unable to control one's emotions
b. know or be able to explain something	e. be unable to do something
c. be unable to think of what to say	f. tell the truth or admit one was wrong

Write sentences using four different idioms from the exercise above.

7. _____

8. _____

9. _____

10. _____

READING STRATEGY | **MAKE INFERENCES** | *Use with textbook page 129.*

REMEMBER When you make inferences, you "read between the lines" to figure out what the author is trying to tell you. Think about what the author has hinted at but not said. Think also of your own experiences.

Read the paragraph. Then answer the questions that follow.

> Aaron and Jim felt they had been sitting there for hours. They could hear the steady sound of their teacher's voice as he gave his account. Once or twice they heard the principal interrupt him. Her voice was loud, but they couldn't make out any words. Aaron tried to catch Jim's eye, but Jim kept staring at his feet. Only his hands moved, twisting constantly. Aaron sighed and leaned back in his chair.

1. Where do you think Aaron and Jim are sitting?

   _____

2. What do you think the teacher is telling the principal?

   _____

3. How do you think Jim is feeling?

   _____

4. What clues in the text help you to infer how Jim is feeling?

   _____

5. How does reading between the lines, or inferring, help you to understand a text?

   _____

   _____

Choose the best answer for each item. Circle the letter of the correct answer.

1. La abuela is _____.

   a. Connie's aunt   **b.** Connie niece   **c.** Connie's grandmother

2. Connie feels embarrassed that Abuela is _____.

   a. the last to leave   **b.** wearing a huge coat   **c.** four feet eleven inches tall
   the airplane

3. Connie doesn't want to take Abuela to _____.

   a. the mall   **b.** school   **c.** church

4. When Abuela cannot find her seat, Connie _____.

   a. hides her face   **b.** hurries to help   **c.** leaves the building

5. Connie does not apologize, but thinks that she has been _____.

   a. right all along   **b.** unkind   **c.** treated badly by her family

RESPONSE TO LITERATURE *Use with textbook page 137.*

This story ends with Connie in her room, thinking about what it feels like to be a zero. Imagine that you are the narrator and you want to apologize to your grandmother. On the following lines, write a letter to your grandmother apologizing for your behavior.

_____

_____

_____

_____

_____

_____

GRAMMAR

***Have to* + Verb** *Use with textbook page 138.*

> **REMEMBER** To express necessity, use *have to* + the base form of a verb.
> **Example:** I have to do my homework.
> The present of *have to* is *have to / has to*. The past is *had to*.
> **Example:** Yesterday, I had to do my homework.
> To form the negative, and express lack of necessity, use *don't / doesn't have to* in the present and *didn't have to* in the past.

Complete the sentences with phrases from the box.

have to visit	has to write	had to clean	don't have to buy	didn't have to go

1. I _____ my grandmother tomorrow because it's her birthday.

2. We _____ to school yesterday because there was a snow storm.

3. We _____ a new car because the one we own is in good condition.

4. After the party last weekend, we _____ the house.

5. He _____ a report for English class by next week.

Complete each sentence with *have to, has to, had to, don't have to,* or *didn't have to* and the verb in parentheses.

6. (feed) When my father was away, I _____ the fish every day.

7. (learn) My sister _____ to drive a car before she can go to college next year.

8. (go) I _____ to the library yesterday because I did research for my science project on the Internet.

9. (remove) We _____ our shoes when we enter the house so that we don't damage the new floor.

10. (wear) The party will be casual, so you _____ a jacket and tie.

WRITING

Write a Personal Narrative *Use with textbook page 139.*

This is the chart that Andrea completed before writing her paragraph.

Who was there	What happened	What was said
My parents and my relatives and I met at Grandpa's house.	We went to the river and swam, played, slept, and cooked. It started raining so we left.	My parents announced, "We are not going to let an aguasero ruin our trip!"

Complete your own three-column chart about a memorable experience you had with a family member or an adventure you had with a friend.

Who was there	What happened	What was said

UNIT 2

How are growth and change related?

READING 5: "Horses and Eagles"

LITERARY ANALYSIS **Influential Authors and Literature**
Use with textbook page 141.

REMEMBER Classical literature is the literature of ancient Greece and Rome. These stories are still popular, and they continue to influence writers of modern literature, television, and movies. Classical works have inspired the literature of many world cultures.

Read the following Summary of Homer's *The Odyssey*. Then answer the question below.

> Odysseus spends ten years trying to return home to his family in Ithaca after the Trojan War ends. In addition to being imprisoned by a nymph for seven years, he encounters a series of obstacles that prevent his returning home. For example, when Odysseus and his men reach the land of the Lotus-eaters, they are fed addictive lotus flowers that make the men forget their desire to return home. Later, a witch named Circe temporarily turns Odysseus's men into pigs. He later fights sea monsters. He also fights and blinds a one-eyed giant, Cyclops. Eventually, after many difficult experiences, Odysseus returns home to his family.

Like *The Odyssey*, many books, television shows, and movies are based on a quest. Usually the main characters encounter unexpected problems while trying to go somewhere, find something, or learn something. Describe the plot of a book, television show, or movie in which one or more characters go on a quest. What obstacles do the characters face? Do they attain their goal?

_____

_____

_____

_____

_____

_____

_____

_____

> **REMEMBER** Authors often tell stories out of time order, using **flashbacks** to describe things that happened before the story takes place. Characterization is the development of a character in a story. An author may use **character foils** to emphasize another character's traits by contrast.

Read the excerpt from a short story below. Circle the section that is a flashback. Then underline the part that reveals a character foil.

Sidef stares hard at the oddly shaped brown case sitting in her closet. The violin sits there, as always, silently waiting for her to bring the music to life.

But the sight of the instrument fills Sidef with dread. Why should she want to play the violin three hours every night, after completing all of her homework? She sits on the bed, wondering what her life would be like if she could play soccer and go to parties and have fun with friends. If only she could be like her sister, Leila, who stayed out of trouble but never obsessed about what her grades were or what her parents thought.

The trouble, Sidef thinks sadly, is that she is good. She remembers the conversation her parents had last fall at the orchestra hall. It was the conversation that had sealed her fate.

The lobby of the orchestra hall was crowded and noisy with the humming of stringed instruments. But the college admissions officer had chased down Sidef's parents. He was a short man with a loud voice. He gushed about her "incredible, wondrous gift for music." "Your daughter," he said, "is headed straight for the top. She can win a scholarship to just about any school she'd like. After that, I'm sure she could play for any orchestra in the entire world."

Her parents beamed at each other, their dreams having nearly come true. Sidef stared at her suede loafers and brown violin case, unable to speak.

Looking back at the conversation now, months later, Sidef realizes that her silence was a huge mistake. After all, she never said a word about wanting to quit. She stares again at the brown case in the closet. How will she ever tell her parents?

LITERARY ANALYSIS   **Literary Devices** *Use with textbook page 143.*

> **REMEMBER** **Irony** is a contrast between appearance and reality. A **paradox** is made up of two statements that seem to have opposite meanings. **Sarcasm** is witty language used to express scorn or disapproval, in which a person may actually say the opposite of what he or she means.

Answer each set of questions below.

1. In the Unit 1 story "Grandmother Spider Brings the Sun," Wolf, Coyote, Possum, and Big Bad Buzzard are all unable to bring the sun. Even though Grandmother Spider is very old and very slow, she succeeds. Why is this an example of irony?

   _____

   _____

The sentences below contain paradoxes. Explain the meaning of each paradox.

Example: In order to be wise, a person must do foolish things.
Explanation: Making mistakes is how we attain wisdom.

2. A seed seems both dead and alive.

   _____

3. A courageous person may be driven by fear.

   _____

4. Sometimes the best thing a person can say is nothing.

   _____

These sentences are examples of sarcasm. Rewrite each sentence in a straightforward manner, restating what the author means.

5. My best friend forgot my birthday again. What a great friend!

   _____

6. Wow, who knew that photosynthesis was such a simple process!

   _____

7. When I crawled out of bed at 5:30 A.M., I felt truly fantastic.

   _____

Using Punctuation for Emphasis *Use with textbook page 148.*

> **REMEMBER** **Quotation marks** may be used to draw the readers' attention to a word or words to show sarcasm or irony. **Dashes** may be used to emphasize information in a sentence that would normally be set off by parentheses.

Write three sentences that express sarcasm or irony for the following situations. Use quotation marks to show the sarcasm or irony. Exchange sentences with a partner and check for correct punctuation.

1. For the third time this week, your brother is an hour late picking you up from school.

_____

_____

2. Your younger sister has borrowed your favorite shirt without asking and torn the sleeve.

_____

_____

3. You spent all weekend creating a great poster for a science project. But on the day you are supposed to present the poster to your class, you realize that you left it on the school bus.

_____

_____

Write three sentences that use dashes to emphasize information that could also be set off by parentheses.

1. _____

_____

2. _____

_____

3. _____

_____

GRAMMAR

Punctuating Clauses, Phrases, and Expressions *Use with textbook page 149.*

> **REMEMBER** **Restrictive clauses** are necessary to make the meaning of the sentence clear. You do not use commas to punctuate restrictive clauses. **Nonrestrictive clauses** are *not* necessary to make the meaning of the sentence clear. They just add more information. Sentences with nonrestrictive clauses are punctuated with commas. Restrictive and nonrestrictive clauses begin with words such as *who*, *which*, and *that*. **Contrasting expressions** clarify what something is by contrasting it with something it is *not*. Sentences with contrasting expressions are punctuated with commas.

Combine each pair of sentences into one sentence. Use the second sentence in each pair as the restrictive relative clause.

1. Here is my favorite pen. It has my initials engraved on it.

   _____

2. Did you see that hockey player? He scored three goals in tonight's game.

   _____

3. Miguel Hernández was a famous poet. He was from Spain.

   _____

The following sentences contain nonrestrictive clauses. Place the comma or commas in the right place for the sentence to make sense.

4. The librarian who has red hair said that she likes to read comic books.

5. Eric's book which was on my desk disappeared.

6. The neighbor who cut down the oak tree thinks that squirrels are pests.

7. The red birdhouse which I made hangs in our backyard.

The following sentences contain contrasting expressions. Place commas in the right places for the sentence to make sense.

8. Miguel Hernández was a famous poet not a novelist from Spain.

9. The librarian with the blonde hair not the red hair helped me find a book.

10. I unlike Marcia prefer pasta to pizza.

Write a Story *Use with textbook pages 150–151.*

REMEMBER A well-told story should contain a variety of literary elements. It needs a developed plot based on interesting, believable characters and a conflict. A feeling of **suspense** can create excitement. The **dialogue** should reveal characters' personalities and situations.

Use this chart to help generate ideas about your characters and the conflict. Write your ideas on the lines.

Who are the main characters in my story?

_____

_____

What happens to the characters in my story? (What's the plot?)

_____

_____

Will the events described in my story appear in the time order in which they occurred? Or will I use devices such as flashback to interrupt the sequence?

_____

_____

How can I use suspense to keep my readers interested?

_____

_____

How will my story's dialogue reveal information about the characters and plot?

_____

_____

_____

WRITING

Write what will happen at each stage of your story in the flowchart below.

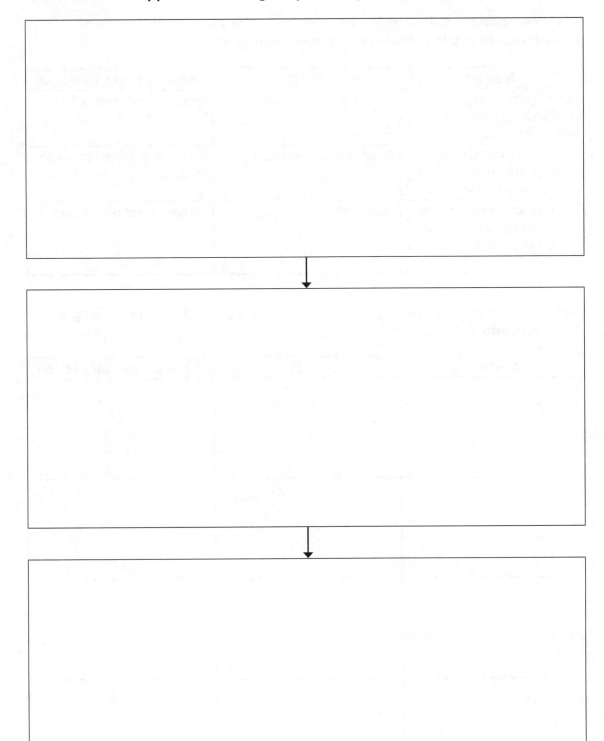

Gather and Organize Information *Use with textbook page 154.*

This is an outline that lists the images and sounds for the introduction to a presentation on making "Horses and Eagles" into a movie.

Speaker	Music	Image on Computer Screen
Hi, we're here to tell you why a great short story can become an even greater movie.	Country and Western music	Photo of a ranch with cattle feeding in the foreground
The story is about how a teen discovers that her parents care about what is important to her.	Sound effects: a horse galloping	Girl sitting at a dinner table with her parents
The story will appeal to a lot of people because we all want to feel understood by the people we love.	Quiet pop song	Girl and parents riding horses

Complete your own outline for the introduction to a presentation on making a short story into a movie.

Speaker	Music	Image on Computer Screen

EDIT AND PROOFREAD   *Use with textbook page 162.*

Read the paragraph carefully. Look for mistakes in spelling, punctuation, and grammar. Correct the mistakes with the editing marks on Student Book page 553. Then rewrite the paragraph correctly on the lines below.

> My friends and i decided to be tourists in our own town and sea all the local attractions. We have wanted to do it all summer. First, we has to find out what the best places are. we went to the tourist bureau. They gave us a list of places to go and a map showing how to got there. We went to the art musuem and took the walking history tour. Finally, we had thirsty so we had a cold drink. Next, we looked at our map again and decided to see won more place. We climbed the observatory, where people used to watch the bay for ships. We enjoyed our day as tourists so much that we Want to do it again soon.

_____

_____

_____

_____

_____

_____

_____

_____

_____

_____

Underline the vocabulary items you know and can use well. Review and practice any you haven't underlined. Underline them when you know them well.

Literary Words	Key Words		Academic Words	
point of view	develop	declined	environment	distribution
plot	embryo	property	function	factors
conflict	germination	residents	potential	migration
characterization	inactive	rural	process	percent
dialogue	protective	trend	affect	region
sarcasm	straighten	urban	anticipation	conduct
			discrimination	ignore
			reaction	instruct
				reluctance

Put a check by the skills you can perform well. Review and practice any you haven't checked off. Check them off when you can perform them well.

Skills	I can . . .
Word Study	☐ recognize and use related words. ☐ recognize and use homographs. ☐ recognize and use long *a, i, o* spelling patterns. ☐ recognize and use idioms.
Reading Strategies	☐ recognize sequence. ☐ compare and contrast. ☐ scan. ☐ make inferences.
Grammar	☐ use sequence words. ☐ use conditional sentences. ☐ use the simple past and present perfect. ☐ use *have to* + verb. ☐ use punctuation for emphasis. ☐ use punctuation for clauses, phrases, and expressions.
Writing	☐ write a story with a starter. ☐ rewrite a familiar story. ☐ write a personal letter. ☐ write a personal narrative. ☐ write a story. ☐ produce a multimedia presentation. ☐ write a fictional narrative.

Visual Literacy: Smithsonian American
Art Museum *Use with textbook pages 164–165.*

LEARNING TO LOOK

Look at *Wheat* by Thomas Hart Benton on page 164 in your textbook. Imagine
that you are from the city on a visit to a farm. You walk through the wheat field
in Benton's painting. Write six things you see in this artwork. State facts, not
opinions.

Example: ___*The wheat is tall.*___

1. _____   4. _____

2. _____   5. _____

3. _____   6. _____

INTERPRETATION

Look at *Untitled (Mixed Flowers)* by Mary Vaux Walcott on page 165 in your
textbook. Answer the following questions.

1. What did Mary Vaux Walcott paint? _____

_____

_____

2. Why do you think she painted it? _____

_____

_____

3. Where do you think Walcott was when she painted *Untitled (Mixed Flowers)*? Describe
the scene.

Example: ___*She was in the mountains.*_____

_____

_____

Look at *Lupin Wedding Crown* by Heikki Seppä on page 165 in your textbook. Use Who, Where, When, What, Why, and How to answer the following questions.

1. (**WHO**) _____
   might wear this bracelet.

2. The artist grew up (**WHERE**) _____
   and saw a wedding ceremony called the Dance of the Crowns, which inspired the design of his bracelet.

3. If you could wear this bracelet, you would wear it (**WHEN**) _____
   _____

4. The (**WHAT**) _____
   of the bracelet is shaped like a honeycomb flower.

5. The artist included an extra loop around the "stem" of the flower tip in his bracelet

   because (**WHY**) _____

6. The artist created the details on the honeycomb flower by (**HOW**) _____
   _____

MEDIA LITERACY

Now that you have read about our place in the natural world and life cycles, go to www.LongmanKeystone.com for links to the Smithsonian website. Follow the online instructions to compare the artwork in your student book with other media that convey similar messages. Which messages are conveyed more directly through visual media? Which ideas are conveyed more effectively through print or audio?

UNIT 3 — How can we tell what's right?

READING 1: "The Golden Serpent"

VOCABULARY **Literary Words** *Use with textbook page 169.*

> **REMEMBER** A **moral** is a lesson taught by a literary work, especially a fable. It is a practical lesson about right and wrong ways to behave. **Example:** Don't put off until tomorrow what you can do today.
> **Motivation** is the reason for a character's actions. **Example:** A character might lie in order to protect someone else.
> The character's motivation for lying, in that case, is to protect someone.

Label each sentence with the literary word it refers to.

Example: _motivation_: They wanted to be friends with her because she was famous.

1. _____: She took off her shoes because they hurt her feet.

2. _____: Beauty is only skin deep.

3. _____: Look before you leap.

4. _____: He avoided talking about school because of his poor grades.

Read "Zian and the Harmonica." Then follow the directions below.

> ### Zian and the Harmonica
>
> Zian had just moved to Sacramento. It was far away from his hometown in China. Zian wanted to fit in with his new classmates, but it was hard. Zian felt terribly alone. So, he found a quiet corner of the cafeteria where he could play his mouth harp in peace.
>
> Zian had always played the instrument whenever he was sad. Playing it now at lunchtime helped. Then one day a few kids listened to Zian's tunes. A day or two later, they asked him questions about the mouth harp. In just a few weeks, Zian and the other students were playing music together. Suddenly Zian had a wonderful group of friends. Zian remembered that his uncle had told him that true friends come to those who are true to themselves. Zian could see now that his uncle was right.

5. Underline the sentences that refer to motivation. Circle a sentence that refers to a moral.

Read the paragraph. Pay attention to the underlined academic words.

> I wanted to get some new curtains for my bedroom, but I couldn't decide what color to choose. I decided to <u>consult</u> my aunt. She's an artist and she's very <u>creative</u>. She came by for dinner last weekend, and I decided to <u>reveal</u> my problem. She suggested bright blue curtains. She said this would <u>contrast</u> nicely with my dark brown carpet. I followed her advice and my new curtains look fantastic.

Write the academic words from the paragraph above next to their correct definitions.

Example: _____*contrast*_____ : a large difference between people or things that are compared

1. _____ : ask for advice from someone who might have the answer

2. _____ : make something known that was previously hidden or unseen

3. _____ : original and inventive

Use the academic words from the paragraph above to complete the sentences.

4. My friend Max comes up with wonderful, _____ ideas.

5. At the end of the story, the author will _____ who committed the crime.

6. She never seems to _____ a teacher for help with homework.

7. It is easy to see the _____ between his writing and mine.

Complete the sentences with your own ideas.

Example: The pale yellow shirt has a nice contrast with

_____*your purple shirt*_____ .

8. I try to be as creative as possible when I _____ .

9. My drawings can reveal _____ .

10. I consult my parents before I _____ .

WORD STUDY Irregular Plurals *Use with textbook page 171.*

REMEMBER Most nouns add an *-s* or *-es* to form their plural. **Example:** *pie/pies* and *hat/hats*.
There are some spelling tips that help figure out when to add *-es* instead of *-s*. Add *-es* to nouns that end in *-s, -z, -x, -sh, -ch*. **Example:** *church/churches* and *kiss/kisses*.
Add *-es* to nouns that end in a consonant plus *-o*. **Example:** *hero/heroes*.
Nouns ending in consonant plus *-y* replace the *-y* with *-i* and add *-es*. **Example:** *story/stories*.
But the *-y* is not replaced if it is preceded by a vowel. **Example:** *donkey/donkeys*.
Nouns ending in *-f* or *-fe* replace the *-f* with *-v* and add *-es*. **Example:** *life/lives*.
There are a few nouns that do not change in the plural. **Example:** *moose*.

Read the words in the box. Then write each word in its plural form in the correct column in the chart.

| elf | knife | box | dog | baby | elephant | witch | key | echo |

Adds *-s*	Ends in *-s, -z, -x, -ch* and adds *-es*
1. 2.	5. 6.
Ends in consonant plus *-y* and replaces *-y* with *-i* and adds *-es*	**Ends in vowel plus *-y* and adds *-s***
3.	7.
Ends in *-o* and adds *-es*	**Ends in *-f* or *-fe* and replaces *-f* with *-v* and adds *-s* or *-es***
4.	8. 9.

Complete the chart with other plural nouns. Use at least one plural per category.

Adds *-s*	Ends in *-s, -z, -x, -ch* and adds *-es*
10.	13.
Ends in consonant plus *-y* and replaces *-y* with *-i* and adds *-es*	**Ends in vowel plus *-y* and adds *-s***
11.	14.
Ends in *-o* and adds *-es*	**Ends in *-f* or *-fe* and replaces *-f* with *-v* and adds *-s* or *-es***
12.	15.

> **REMEMBER** Identifying problems and solutions helps you understand a text better.

Read each passage and answer the questions.

> Jessica was thrilled. Her friend Cathy had got them tickets to a concert in the city on November 1. After the concert, they planned to go out to dinner. When Jessica informed her mother of her plans, her Mom said "Any other day would be fine. But November 1 is el Dia de los Muertos. It is a special day. We must spend it together as a family."
>
> Jessica replied, "Mom, I am just too old for another family holiday. I'm a teenager and I need my independence. I'm going to the concert whether you like it or not."

1. What is the problem in the passage above?

_____

2. What is a possible solution to the problem in the passage above?

_____

> Later that day, Jessica explained the problem to Cathy. Jessica said, "I feel really badly about missing el Dia de los Muertos. It doesn't begin until 5:00 P.M., but since we're having dinner we won't get home until after 9:00 P.M."
>
> Cathy said, "I have a great idea. The concert should be over by 3:00 P.M. We can come straight home after the concert. We'll miss having dinner after the concert, but at least this way, you'll get home in time for the celebrations of el Dia de los Muertos."
>
> Jessica shared the idea with her mother. Her mother kissed her on the forehead and said, "I knew you would do the right thing."

3. What is the problem in the passage above?

_____

4. What is the solution in the passage above?

_____

5. Do you think the solution is good? Why or why not?

_____

COMPREHENSION *Use with textbook page 178.*

Choose the best answer for each item. Circle the letter of the correct answer.

1. People sent Pundabi loaves of bread because _____.

   a. they had too much bread
   b. he was hungry
   c. there were questions inside that they needed answered

2. The king wanted to _____.

   a. see if Pundabi was a fraud
   b. put Pundabi in jail
   c. pay Pundabi well

3. Pundabi took the king to the market and the village to _____.

   a. buy food for the king
   b. show the king his people
   c. find gold coins

4. Pundabi knew that the king's people didn't steal the Golden Serpent because they _____.

   a. had gold and rubies
   b. had lots of bread
   c. had very few things

5. To find the Golden Serpent, Pundabi told the king to _____.

   a. count to a hundred
   b. pay Pundabi with gold coins
   c. give gold to his people

RESPONSE TO LITERATURE *Use with textbook page 179.*

Think about what will happen when the king opens his eyes and doesn't find the Golden Serpent. Write about what his reaction will be.

_____

_____

_____

_____

_____

_____

The Modal _must_ _Use with textbook page 180._

> **REMEMBER** The modal _must_ expresses necessity and obligation.
> **Example:** You must breathe in order to stay alive.
> The modal _must_ can also be used to speculate, or make guesses, about the present and the past.
> **Example:** You must have studied hard in fifth grade.

Read each sentence below. Write _N_ on the line if the sentence expresses a necessity. Write _O_ on the line if the sentence expresses an obligation. Write _S-Present_ if the sentence expresses a speculation or a guess about something in the present. Write _S-Past_ if the sentence expresses a speculation, or a guess about something in the past.

_____ 1. Every animal must have food of some kind in order to survive.

_____ 2. You must work hard if you want to do well in school.

_____ 3. Megan must be about ten years old now.

_____ 4. Dad must have been thrilled when he got that job three years ago.

_____ 5. Crows must build a nest before the female can lay her eggs.

Use the correct combination of _must_ and a verb to express each idea in parentheses.

Example: (the speculation or guess that Alex graduated from middle school)
      Alex must have graduated from middle school.

6. (the speculation or guess that Jennifer can speak Spanish)

_____

7. (the necessity to carry an umbrella if it is raining)

_____

8. (the obligation, or duty of wishing a friend a happy birthday)

_____

9. (the obligation, or duty to visit a friend who is ill)

_____

10. (the speculation or guess that Alicia was two years old when she had chicken pox)

_____

WRITING

Write a Review *Use with textbook page 181.*

This is the graphic organizer that Dylan completed before writing his paragraph.

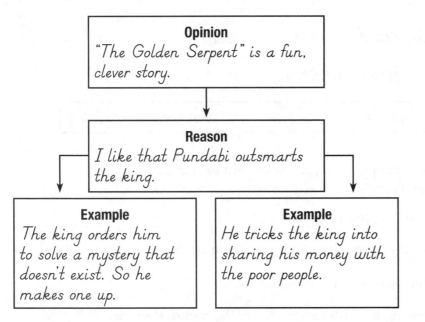

Opinion
"The Golden Serpent" is a fun, clever story.

↓

Reason
I like that Pundabi outsmarts the king.

Example
The king orders him to solve a mystery that doesn't exist. So he makes one up.

Example
He tricks the king into sharing his money with the poor people.

Complete your own graphic organizer for a review of a story, book, movie, or television show.

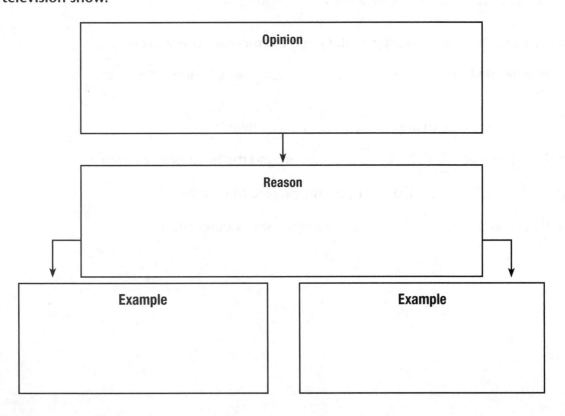

Opinion

Reason

Example

Example

VOCABULARY **Key Words** *Use with textbook page 183.*

Write each word in the box next to its definition.

astronomy	celestial	eccentric	proposed	revolution	terrestrial

Example: *revolution* : one complete circular movement or spin around a central point

1. _____ : deviating from a circular path

2. _____ : officially suggested that something be done

3. _____ : the science of the stars and planets

4. _____ : relating to Earth rather than to the moon, stars, or other planets

5. _____ : relating to the sky or heaven

Use the words in the box at the top of the page to complete the sentences.

6. My uncle decided to study _____ because he likes to look at the stars.

7. Plants that grow on Earth are _____ plants.

8. The basketball made a _____ around the hoop before falling in.

9. She _____ that we begin the project after lunch.

10. Objects that are _____ are in the sky or outer space.

VOCABULARY **Academic Words** *Use with textbook page 184.*

Read the paragraph. Pay attention to the underlined academic words.

> In the past few years, there has been much <u>debate</u> over whether or not Pluto should be called a planet. In 2006, scientists got together to <u>define</u> the traits of a planet. Based on their definition, Pluto was no longer a real planet. Some people find it hard to think <u>objectively</u> about Pluto, and are upset about this. They are probably <u>biased</u> because Pluto has been called a planet since it was first discovered in 1930.

Write the letter of the correct definition next to each word.

Example: __*b*__ define

_____ 1. objectively

_____ 2. debate

_____ 3. biased

a. in a way that is not influenced by a person's feelings, beliefs, or ideas

b. clearly show what something is or means

c. unfair because of a preference or dislike of something

d. formal discussion of a subject in which people express differing opinions

Use the academic words from the exercise above to complete the sentences.

4. Students held a _____ about whether they should have homework over the school vacation.

5. Our teacher tried to _____ the word *verdad* in English.

6. Since Alejandro is my brother, anything I say about him is likely to be

   _____.

7. Whenever I think about a problem, I try to look at it _____.

Complete the sentences with your own ideas.

Example: I define opinions as *what a person thinks or believes* .

8. The topic I would most love to debate is _____.

9. One subject I might be very biased about is _____.

10. It is important to think objectively about issues facing our country because

   _____.

> **REMEMBER** A prefix is a letter or group of letters added to the beginning of a word to change its meaning. For example, the prefix *un-* means "not." When you add *un-* to *happy*, the new word is *unhappy*, the opposite of *happy*. The prefix *inter-* means between or among and *re-* means again in a new way. Knowing just a few prefixes can help you figure out many unfamiliar words.

Look at the chart below. Add the prefix *inter-*, *un-*, or *re-* as directed to create a new word. Write the new word on the chart. Then write the meaning.

Word	Prefix	New Word	Definition
1. office	*inter-*	interoffice	Between offices in a company
2. city	*inter-*		
3. coastal	*inter-*		
4. finished	*un-*		
5. familiar	*un-*		
6. grateful	*un-*		
7. solved	*re-*		
8. heat	*re-*		
9. fuel	*re-*		

Create a new word by adding the prefix *inter-*, *un-*, or *re-* to each word below. Check a dictionary if needed. Then write the definition next to the new word.

Example: scrupulous ___unscrupulous___   *not principled*

10. mural _____

11. thinkable _____

12. grade _____

13. successful _____

14. name _____

15. planetary _____

READING STRATEGY | **DISTINGUISH FACT FROM OPINION**

Use with textbook page 185.

> **REMEMBER** Facts are something that can be proven, or are true. An opinion is what someone believes or thinks.

Read each paragraph below and underline the facts.

1. The planet Pluto was named on March 24, 1930. Pluto got its name in an interesting way. Amateur astronomer Clyde Tombaugh discovered the planet. He worked at the Lowell Observatory.

2. The Lowell Observatory was given the right to name the planet. The widow of the founder of Lowell Observatory suggested her own first name, Constance. However, the director of the observatory didn't want to use that name.

Read each paragraph below. Underline the facts and draw circles around the opinions.

3. Meanwhile, an eleven-year-old English girl named Venetia Burney thought the name Pluto would be a good choice for the cold, distant planet. That is because Pluto was the Roman name for the god of the cold, dark underworld.

4. Venetia was smart. She suggested the name to her grandfather, Falconer Madan. He told a professor about Venetia's suggestion. The professor told it to the Lowell Observatory. The Lowell Observatory agreed to name the planet Pluto.

5. How can the skill of distinguishing between fact and opinion help you to understand what you read?

   _____

   _____

   _____

Choose the best answer for each item. Circle the letter of the correct answer.

1. The author says that his love for Pluto is _____.

   a. personal   **b.** nonexistent   **c.** half-formed

2. The tone of "I Love Pluto" is _____.

   a. serious   **b.** humorous   **c.** angry

3. Pluto is compared to _____.

   a. a moon   **b.** a Homecoming Queen   **c.** a girl in black who writes poems

4. Pluto has a very eccentric _____.

   a. orbit   **b.** color   **c.** history

5. The author wants Pluto to be considered _____.

   a. a planet   **b.** an asteroid   **c.** a moon

EXTENSION *Use with textbook page 191.*

Write the name of a planet that interests you most. Then research the planet and complete the graphic organizer below.

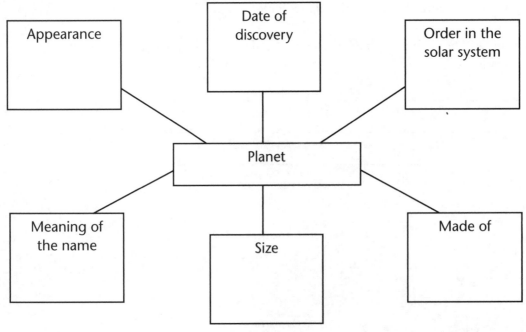

GRAMMAR

Some **and Indefinite Pronouns** *Use with textbook page 192.*

> **REMEMBER** *Some* and indefinite pronouns are used to make generalizations. *Some* is always plural and can be used as an adjective or a pronoun. Indefinite pronouns include words such as *everything, everyone, anything* and *nothing*. These singular indefinite pronouns take singular verbs and singular personal pronouns.
> **Example:** Nothing is wrong. Some (athletes) spend hours in the morning training. (Note that when *some* is used alone as an indefinite pronoun, it is plural.)

Circle the correct indefinite pronoun in each sentence below.

Example: (Everybody) / Nobody knows that Earth has only one moon.

1. Scientists know a lot about the planets, but they do not know anything / everything about them.

2. Anyone / Someone can see that Peter wants to be class president.

3. Because it is so far away, everyone / no one was able to see Uranus before the invention of the telescope.

4. Some / Something happened 65 million years ago that caused the dinosaurs to die; perhaps an asteroid crashed into the Yucatán Peninsula.

5. Venus is so hot that scientists think nothing / something can live there.

Write a sentence with each indefinite pronoun in parentheses. Use a singular verb with indefinite pronouns that begin with *every, any,* and *no*. Use a plural verb with *some* when it appears alone as an indefinite pronoun.

Example: (anyone) _Anyone who studies the solar system learns about Pluto._

6. (everyone) _____

7. (some) _____

8. (anything) _____

9. (nobody) _____

10. (everything) _____

Write a Letter to the Editor *Use with textbook page 193.*

This is the word web that Ruth completed before writing her paragraph.

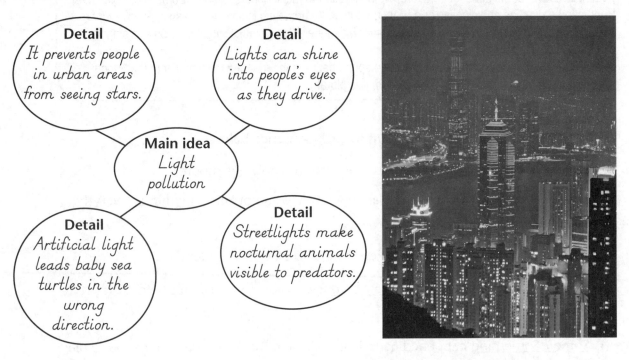

Detail
It prevents people in urban areas from seeing stars.

Detail
Lights can shine into people's eyes as they drive.

Main idea
Light pollution

Detail
Artificial light leads baby sea turtles in the wrong direction.

Detail
Streetlights make nocturnal animals visible to predators.

Complete your own word web for a letter to the editor of a newspaper, magazine or other publication about a problem in your community or school.

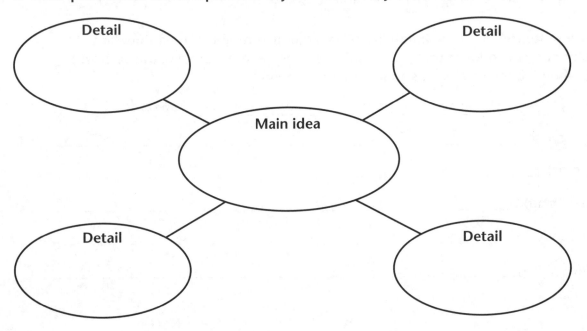

Detail

Detail

Main idea

Detail

Detail

Name _____ Date _____

How can we tell what's right?

READING 3: From *A Single Shard*

VOCABULARY **Literary Words** *Use with textbook page 195.*

REMEMBER A conflict is a struggle between opposing forces. An **internal conflict** is a conflict within a character. The **theme** of a work of fiction is its central idea or message.

Label each sentence with the literary word it refers to.

Example: *internal conflict*   She couldn't decide what to eat for dinner.

1. _____   He couldn't decide whether to concentrate on sports or music.

2. _____   The book is really about the relationship between people and nature.

3. _____   The story is about global warming.

Read the story "Most Valuable Player" below. Then answer the questions below.

Most Valuable Player

Mary and Gemma both wanted the Most Valuable Player award, but only one of them could win. Mary was a great athlete, but it was Gemma who scored most of the goals.

At the end of the final game, Gemma missed a goal. Mary ran down the field, kicked the ball, and scored a goal. Now Coach Smith had a problem. Mary had won the game, but Gemma had scored most of the goals all year. After struggling with the problem, he gave the award to Gemma. It was the fair thing to do.

4. What are the examples of conflict in the passage above?

_____

_____

5. What is the theme or central idea of the passage above?

_____

_____

Read the paragraph below. Pay attention to the underlined academic words.

Elisa found a lost dog. She wanted to keep him, but she couldn't <u>justify</u> this without first searching for the owner. It would go against her <u>principles</u> to keep the dog if he belonged to someone else. She took a step back to <u>analyze</u> the situation. She decided to put up flyers near where she found the dog. In the end, Elisa found the owner, and was glad she had been <u>ethical</u>.

Write the academic words from the paragraph above next to their correct definitions.

Example: _____*ethical*_____: having to do with right and wrong

1. _____: examine or think about something carefully in order to understand it

2. _____: a moral or set of ideas that makes you behave in a certain way

3. _____: give a reasonable or acceptable explanation for something

Use the academic words from the paragraph above to complete the sentences.

4. I live by the _____ that a good education is essential for success.

5. Every day I _____ my homework assignments to plan what to do first.

6. It is not _____ to cheat on a test.

7. I can usually _____ my grades by thinking of how much I study.

Complete the sentences with your own ideas.

Example: A good principle is to _____*treat other people the way you want to be treated*_____.

8. My teacher often asks me to analyze _____.

9. I can justify spending money on _____ because _____.

10. My parents believe it is ethical to _____.

Name _____ Date _____

REMEMBER The vowel combination *ea* most often stands for the long *e* sound as in *jeans*. It can also stand for the long *a* sound, as in *steak*, and for the short *e* sound as in *bread*.

Read the words in the box. They each contain the vowel combination *ea*. Sort the words depending on the sound the vowel team stands for in the chart.

~~neat~~	dream	health	great	ready	spread	peach	peace

Long *e*	Long *a*	Short *e*
neat	4.	5.
1.		6.
2.		7.
3.		

Circle the words with an *ea* vowel combination. Then write sentences using the words.

Example: red, (read,) rate ___*I read two books last year.*_____

8. deed, dead, dad _____

9. angel, break, eight _____

10. lead, led, late _____

11. meat, feet, berry _____

12. coffee, sleep, speak _____

13. red, head, be _____

14. at, eat, rate _____

15. weak, week, wake _____

Use with textbook page 197.

REMEMBER An author's purpose is his or her reason for writing, such as to entertain, inform, or persuade. Identifying an author's purpose will help you better analyze a text.

Read each paragraph and give the author's purpose.

1. This note is to tell you about some changes to the library system. The library's new hours will be 9 A.M. to 5 P.M. Monday through Saturday and 10 A.M. to 6 P.M. on Sundays.

   What is the author's purpose? _____

2. The manatee is in danger of dying out. Encourage members of Congress to support laws to stop boating in areas where manatees live. Tell your representatives to create safe places for manatees and other wildlife.

   What is the author's purpose? _____

3. Whooping cranes do a mating dance,
   Which is worth seeing if you get the chance.
   They court by making strange sounds,
   And flap their wings and leap around.

   What is the author's purpose? _____

4. You must visit the Arkansas National Wildlife Refuge. It is one of the best places to see nature. Plan to visit the refuge late in the winter. The beauty of the park will astound you!

   What is the author's purpose? _____

5. The only child of Carl and Candy Crane, Kris had lived in Wood Buffalo National Park for as long as he could remember. This year, however, his wings were strong and he would make his first flight south for the winter. Kris could hardly wait!

   What is the author's purpose? _____

COMPREHENSION   *Use with textbook page 202.*

Choose the best answer for each item. Circle the letter of the correct answer.

1. Tree-ear's fortune was a _____.

   a. bag of rice   **b.** a backpack   **c.** a walking crutch

2. Tree-ear knew that the rice in the *jiggeh* was from last year because _____.

   a. there was a   **b.** rice trickled through   **c.** this season's rice
   woven-straw box   a hole in the   had just begun
   on the *jiggeh*   straw box   to grow

3. The words that tell about Tree-ear's conflict are _____.

   a. "oblivious, the man   **b.** "Tree-ear's thoughts   **c.** "Tree-ear had learned
   continued on   wrestled with   from Crane-man's
   his way"   one another"   example"

4. The man with the *jiggeh* lost some of his rice because _____.

   a. Crane-man took it   **b.** he dropped his *jiggeh*   **c.** he was impatient

5. The author's purpose for this selection is to _____.

   a. entertain   **b.** inform   **c.** persuade

RESPONSE TO LITERATURE   *Use with textbook page 203.*

Imagine a different response from the man with the *jiggeh*. Write a new ending to the story.

_____

_____

_____

_____

_____

_____

_____

The Uses of *would* *Use with textbook page 204.*

> **REMEMBER** Use *would* + the base form of a verb to express the future in the past.
> **Example:** She thought he would have dinner ready when she got home.
> *Would* is also used in implied conditions. **Example:** I would have gone if the movie were playing.
> Use *would* + *rather* to state a preference. **Example:** I would rather get a ride home than take the bus.

Complete each sentence with a phrase from the box.

would rather eat	would be	would have used	would rather grow	would cook

1. The farmer _____ wheat than rice.

2. We knew that sushi _____ popular with young people.

3. They _____ rice with their dinner than corn.

4. My father _____ chopsticks to eat the rice.

5. The chef _____ rice in a rice cooker every night.

Write sentences with your own ideas.

Example: I would have made _lunch if there were time._____

6. I thought my friend would _____

7. I would rather eat _____

8. I would have worn _____

9. I'd rather visit _____

10. I knew that everyone would _____

Name _____ Date _____

Writing a Persuasive Paragraph *Use with textbook page 205.*

This is the T-chart that Jessica completed before writing her paragraph.

Pros	Cons
If Tree-ear waits to tell the farmer, he might end up with more rice. Telling the farmer right away would make Tree-ear feel good.	People might think it's dishonest, like stealing. Tree-ear's stomach would be empty.

Complete your own T-chart for a persuasive paragraph on a topic or question you feel strongly about.

Pros	Cons

How can we tell what's right?

READING 4: "Marian Anderson: A Voice for Change"

VOCABULARY   **Key Words** *Use with textbook page 207.*

Write each word in the box next to its definition.

auditorium	concert	congregation	determination	injustice	spirituals

Example: ___*concert*___: a performance given by musicians or singers

1. _____: a situation in which people are treated very unfairly

2. _____: a large building used for concerts or public meetings

3. _____: religious songs first sung by enslaved African Americans in the United States

4. _____: a group of people gathered in a church for a religious service, or the people who usually go to a particular church

5. _____: the quality of trying to do something even when it is difficult

Use the words in the box at the top of the page to complete the sentences.

6. Every Sunday, the church _____ gathered to sing and pray.

7. The people met in a large _____ that they used as a church.

8. They loved singing _____ more than any other kind of music.

9. Their songs often spoke of the _____ the people suffered.

10. The people sang to show their _____ to overcome prejudice.

Name _____ Date _____

Read the paragraph. Pay attention to the underlined academic words.

> Rosa Parks is well-known for her refusal to give up her bus seat to a white man. She chose to <u>pursue</u> justice at a time when African Americans did not have equal rights. Rosa's brave stand focused attention on the <u>issue</u> of racial inequality. As a single <u>individual</u>, she inspired many people to protest unfair laws. Her contribution to the civil rights movement was an important <u>achievement</u>.

Write the letter of the correct definition next to each word.

Example: ___*d*___ issue

_____ **1.** individual

_____ **2.** pursue

_____ **3.** achievement

a. continue doing an activity or trying to achieve something over a long time

b. person considered separately from other people in the same group

c. something important you succeed in doing as a result of your actions

d. a subject, problem, or question that people discuss

Use the academic words from the exercise above to complete the sentences.

4. My father told me to _____ a worthwhile career.

5. He said that winning the Nobel Prize was a major _____.

6. They debated the _____ of whom to vote for in the next election.

7. Every _____ must decide on his or her own career.

Complete the sentences with your own ideas.

Example: Each individual ___*will choose a favorite topic*___.

8. A career I would like to pursue is _____.

9. I think my proudest achievement is _____.

10. An issue I'd like to discuss is _____.

REMEMBER Synonyms are two or more words that have similar meanings.
Examples: *begin/start, find/locate.*

Look at the words in the first column of the chart. Write a synonym for each word in the second column.

Word	Synonym	Word	Synonym
quiet	*silent*	4. mistake	
1. attempt		5. considerate	
2. gift		6. terrify	
3. huge		7. end	

Rewrite the sentences using a synonym for the underlined word.

Example: You will have to <u>split</u> the work fairly.

   You will have to divide the work fairly.

8. I will <u>perform</u> in a theatrical production.

_____

9. The reviews of the play were <u>great</u>.

_____

10. The stage was very <u>small</u>.

_____

11. He worked the lights for the <u>whole</u> performance.

_____

12. They will not have to <u>postpone</u> the opening of the show.

_____

13. We had to <u>donate</u> a few dollars to the program.

_____

14. She is a very <u>thin</u> person.

_____

15. All of my answers were <u>right</u>.

_____

READING STRATEGY | **SUMMARIZE** | *Use with textbook page 209.*

> **REMEMBER** When you summarize, you restate the main ideas of a text in your own words.

Read the paragraphs below. Then summarize each paragraph and answer the question.

1. When Bessie Smith was born, no one would have predicted that she would become an empress one day. Her parents died before she was nine. To help support her family, Bessie Smith sang and danced in the street for money.

   Summarize the paragraph in your own words.

   _____

2. One day Bessie's older brother Clarence came to town with a performance group known as "Ma" Rainey's Rabbit Foot Minstrels. Soon, she became part of the group, too. They were a big success. In 1923, Bessie Smith made her first recording, "Downhearted Blues."

   Summarize the paragraph in your own words.

   _____

3. The song was a huge hit and started Smith's career with a bang. People started calling Bessie Smith the "Empress of the Blues." She performed with many of the great jazz musicians of the time. She even starred in a film in 1929.

   Summarize the paragraph in your own words.

   _____

4. The Depression, a time of economic hardship for many Americans, greatly affected musicians, including Bessie Smith. Few people could afford to pay to hear them perform. In 1933, however, Smith began a comeback.

   Summarize the paragraph in your own words.

   _____

5. How can the skill of summarizing help you to understand what you read?

   _____

Choose the best answer for each item. Circle the letter of the correct answer.

1. Marian Anderson had private singing teachers because _____.

    a. she didn't want to go to school   **b.** segregated singing schools would not accept her   **c.** her parents insisted

2. To sing professionally, Marian needed _____.

    a. training   **b.** church   **c.** permission

3. Marian went to Europe to _____.

    a. sing spirituals   **b.** learn German operas   **c.** perfect her language skills

4. Because she disagreed with the DAR's decision, Eleanor Roosevelt _____.

    a. turned to the local school board   **b.** ended her membership with DAR   **c.** joined the NAACP

5. Marian's most historic performance took place at the Lincoln Memorial

because _____.

    a. segregated auditoriums would not let her sing   **b.** everyplace else was booked   **c.** it was her first choice

EXTENSION *Use with textbook page 215.*

Research another musician who interests you. In the space below, write a summary of his or her career.

_____

_____

_____

_____

_____

GRAMMAR

Superlative Adjectives *Use with textbook page 216.*

> **REMEMBER** Superlative adjectives are used to compare three or more things. Superlative adjectives generally come before the nouns they modify.
> **Example:** The blue house on Lakeview Road is the *largest* house in the city.

Circle the correct form of the superlative adjective in each sentence below.

Example: That is the (dirtiest)/ most dirty kitchen I have ever seen.

1. The <u>expensivest / most expensive</u> watch was the one he wanted.

2. The man who was hollering was the <u>angriest / angryest</u> customer I've ever seen.

3. The <u>best / bestest</u> student in the class won a scholarship.

4. I watched the <u>interestingest / most interesting</u> program on TV last night.

5. My grandmother was the <u>oldest / most old</u> person in the room.

Write sentences with the superlative form of the adjective in parentheses.

Example: (calm) *The lake is calmest when there is no wind.*

6. (beautiful) _____

7. (bright) _____

8. (lazy) _____

9. (terrible) _____

10. (sweet) _____

11. (bad) _____

12. (tiny) _____

13. (soft) _____

14. (terrifying) _____

15. (loud) _____

Write an Advertisement *Use with textbook page 217.*

This is the word web that Jessica completed before writing her paragraph.

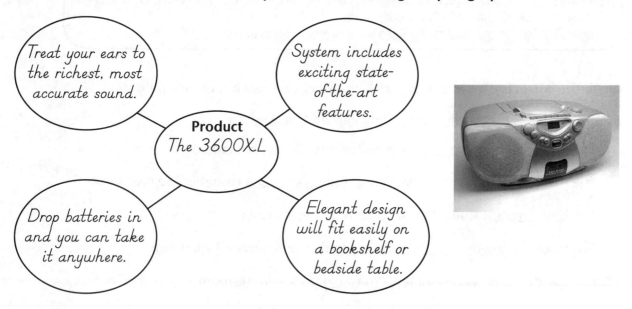

Complete your own word web for an ad about a product, event, singer, or artist.

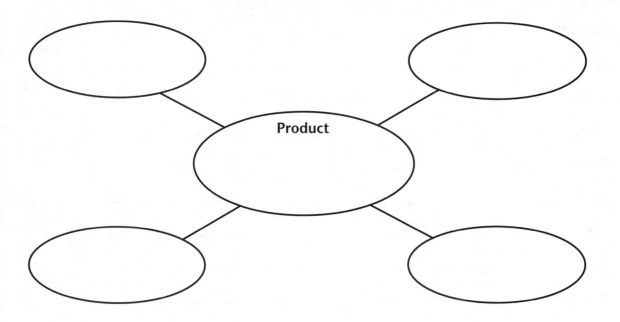

Name _____ Date _____

How can we tell what's right?

READING 5: "Helmet Laws" and "High School Student Uniforms"

VOCABULARY **Word Study: Analogies** *Use with textbook page 219.*

REMEMBER An **analogy** shows a relationship between a pair of words. Analogies can draw comparisons between ideas or between the function of objects. Colons are often used to show an analogy.

Look at the chart below. Identify the relationship between the pair of words in the first column. Then fill in a word that completes the analogy in the second column.

Words	Analogy
Example ring : finger	earring : _ear_
1. slow : turtle	_____ : race car
2. sun : warmth	snow : _____
3. dog : fur	person : _____
4. ship : ocean	airplane : _____
5. car : pollution	fireplace : _____
6. thread : clothing	mortar : _____
7. pencil : write	keyboard : _____

> **REMEMBER** An **author's purpose** is his or her reason for writing. An author can write to **inform**, **entertain**, or **persuade**. To determine the author's purpose, a reader should consider the details, style, tone, and diction (or word choice) of the selection.

Read the following passages. For each passage, determine whether the author's purpose was to inform, entertain, or persuade. Write *I* on the blank line if the purpose is to inform, *E* if the purpose is to entertain, or *P* if the purpose is to persuade.

_____ 1. "When light strikes an object, the light can be reflected, or bounced off the object. The light might also be absorbed, or taken in by the object."—from *Light,* Unit 1

_____ 2. "People in the United States move often. According to the United States Census Bureau, 40.1 million Americans. . . changed residence between March 2002 and March 2003."—from *Migration Patterns,* Unit 2

_____ 3. "'You made me feel like a zero, like a nothing,' she says in Spanish, *un cero, nada.* She is trembling, an angry little old woman lost in a heavy winter coat. . . ."—from *Abuela Invents the Zero,* Unit 2

_____ 4. "I left the amusement park that night with a new appreciation for the things I take for granted. . . . Every day I realize all over again that everything in the world is beautiful—you just need the light to be able to see it."—from *Summer Light,* Unit 1

_____ 5. "Whenever possible, people should use canvas bags to carry their groceries. Both paper and plastic grocery bags create environmental problems."

TEXT ANALYSIS **Substantiated and Unsubstantiated**
Opinions *Use with textbook page 221.*

> **REMEMBER** A **substantiated opinion** is one that is based on fact. An **unsubstantiated opinion** is one that cannot be proven or backed up by facts.

Read the following sentences. For each sentence, state whether the speaker's opinion is substantiated or unsubstantiated. In the blank by each sentence, write *S* **for substantiated or** *U* **for unsubstantiated.**

_____ 1. The government should make it easier for college students to get loans to pay for tuition. After all, the newspaper said last week that it's gotten more difficult for students to get loans in the last decade.

_____ 2. No one likes to pay taxes, so we shouldn't have to pay them anymore! The federal tax forms are confusing and too long.

_____ 3. I think cafeteria lunches taste bad, so the school board should revise the menus.

_____ 4. The politician should resign—there are just too many ugly rumors about him. What are the odds that he's honest?

_____ 5. I think it's best to drive small cars, since research shows that these cars are the safest and most reliable.

_____ 6. Students who want to make high grades shouldn't spend any time watching television or playing video games during the week.

_____ 7. Recycling is a waste of time. I don't believe all that plastic ever gets made into anything. The city probably just puts recyclables with all the other trash.

_____ 8. It was really cold last winter. To me, this means that global warming can't be real.

> **REMEMBER** There are many tools that writers and speakers use to persuade their audiences. To give their writing a musical quality, they often use **alliteration** (the repetition of sounds at the beginning of words). To create emphasis, they often **repeat** a word or phrase. Writers and speakers also use **figurative language** to create an emotional effect.

Read the excerpt below. It is from a speech that Patrick Henry gave in 1775. He was trying to persuade the American colonists that they needed to go to war with Britain. Use a dictionary to look up any words you don't know. Then answer the questions below.

---

from Patrick Henry's 1775 speech
"Give Me Liberty or Give Me Death"

Let us not, I beseech you, sir, deceive ourselves. Sir, we have done everything that could be done to avert the storm which is now coming on. We have petitioned; we have remonstrated; we have supplicated. . . . There is no longer any room for hope.

. . .

Why stand we here idle? What is it that gentlemen wish? What would they have? Is life so dear, or peace so sweet, as to be purchased at the price of chains and slavery? Forbid it, Almighty God! I know not what course others may take; but as for me, give me liberty or give me death!

---

1. Where does Henry use repetition? _____

   _____ .

2. A section that uses alliteration is _____

   _____ .

3. An example of figurative language is _____

   _____ .

GRAMMAR

Reciprocal Pronouns *Use with textbook page 228.*

> **REMEMBER** **Reciprocal pronouns** are used to show a mutual, or two-way, action or feeling. There are two main reciprocal pronouns: *each other* and *one another.* Use *each other* when talking or writing about two people or animals. Use *one another* when talking or writing about more than two people or animals.

Complete each sentence with the correct reciprocal pronoun.

1. The two best friends never argued with _____.

2. Over the summer, Ricardo, Jeanne, and Keisha did not see _____.

3. The four playful puppies chased _____ through the yard.

4. My mother taught all of us to be kind to _____.

5. The representatives in Washington frequently disagreed with _____.

6. The high school sweethearts were obviously deeply in love with

   _____.

7. The teacher asked Brad and me to share our textbook with _____.

8. The two parakeets seemed to be calling out to _____.

9. In kindergarten we were taught to be friendly to _____.

10. Betsy and Ani wore the same shoe size, so they often swapped shoes with

    _____.

Subjunctive Mood *Use with textbook page 229.*

> **REMEMBER** Verbs in the **subjunctive mood** express conditions that do not currently exist. The subjective mood is used to express things such as wishes, doubts, possibilities, as well as other situations that are unlikely or untrue.

Read each sentence below. If the subjunctive mood is used correctly, write C. If it is incorrect, write I. Then rewrite the incorrect sentences using the subjunctive mood.

1. I wish I was taller. _____

2. If Saul was to join the swim team, I would probably join too. _____

    _____

3. The teacher insists that Walter arrives on time to class. _____

    _____

4. I doubted you were coming. _____

5. Maria wished that she was going to the dance. _____

    _____

6. Dr. Luis suggested that my grandmother be on a healthier diet. _____

    _____

7. If it was I, I'd choose the red one. _____

    _____

8. If she was wise, she would study more for the geometry test. _____

    _____

9. Jake doubted whether Bo was really his friend. _____

    _____

10. No one would be angry with you if you were just a little more patient. _____

    _____

WRITING

Write a Persuasive Essay *Use with textbook pages 230–231.*

REMEMBER The **structure** of your persuasive paragraph is important. The **thesis statement** states the point of your paragraph. It is the most important thing, and it often comes first. A well-structured paragraph will also have **details** that support your thesis statement.

In the chart below, make up a thesis statement about a topic. Write details that support your opinion.

Topic or Issue:

Evidence and Details:
1.

2.

3.

4.

My Thoughts:
1.

2.

3.

Thesis Statement:

Edit and Proofread *Use with textbook page 233.*

Read the paragraph below carefully. Look for mistakes in spelling, punctuation, and grammar. Correct the mistakes with proofreaders' marks on Student Book page 553. Then rewrite the paragraph correctly on the lines below.

> The local city council should pass a law on recycling electronic devices. Currently, our city has about 5,000 computers, cell phones, and television thrown away each year. Electronix contain chemicals that are very dangurous to the environment and to humans. Recently, scientists found the high levels of mercury, cadmium, and other dangerous metals in our local landfill. Studies show that electronic waste can damage human lungs, too. It's important that they these materials be recycled properly, so that we can reuse the materails instead of polluting the environment.

_____

_____

_____

_____

_____

_____

_____

_____

_____

Unit 3

EDIT AND PROOFREAD *Use with textbook page 240.*

Read the paragraph below carefully. Look for mistakes in spelling, punctuation, and grammar. Correct the mistakes with the editing marks on Student Book page 553. Then rewrite the paragraph correctly on the lines below.

> Have you ever wondered why Schools start so early in the morning? Most high schools start around 8:00 A.M. and some even start as early as 7am. What I don't understand is why schools need to start so early Studies show that adolescents grow a lot in the early morning hours. That is why we feel so tired when we get up early in the morning. we really should be fast asleep! It would be wiser to let us sleep until 8 or 9 o'clock in the morning And start school at 10 o'clock in the morning. That would give our bodies time to grow and let our minds take a nice long rest before starting the school day.
>
> Some high schools in new York start school at 10:00 A.M. and i have heard that their students are much happyer and better rested

_____

_____

_____

_____

_____

_____

_____

_____

_____

Underline the vocabulary items you know and can use well. Review and practice any you haven't underlined. Underline them when you know them well.

Literary Words	Key Words		Academic Words	
moral	astronomy	auditorium	consult	analyze
motivation	celestial	concert	contrast	ethical
internal conflict	eccentric	congregation	creative	justify
theme	proposed	determination	reveal	principle
	revolution	injustice	biased	achievement
	terrestrial	spirituals	debate	individual
			define	issue
			objectively	pursue

Put a check by the skills you can perform well. Review and practice any you haven't checked off. Check them off when you can perform them well.

Skills	I can . . .
Word Study	☐ recognize and spell irregular plurals. ☐ recognize and use prefixes. ☐ recognize and spell words with long and short vowels. ☐ recognize and use synonyms. ☐ recognize and use analogies.
Reading Strategies	☐ identify problems and solutions. ☐ distinguish fact from opinion. ☐ identify author's purpose. ☐ summarize.
Grammar	☐ use the modal *must*. ☐ use *some* and indefinite pronouns. ☐ use *would* correctly. ☐ use superlative adjectives correctly. ☐ use reciprocal pronouns. ☐ use subjunctive mood.
Writing	☐ write a review. ☐ write a letter to the editor. ☐ write a persuasive paragraph. ☐ write an advertisement. ☐ write a persuasive essay. ☐ write a speech.

Visual Literacy: Smithsonian American
Art Museum *Use with textbook pages 242–243.*

LEARNING TO LOOK

Look at *Monekana* by Deborah Butterfield on page 242. Write down four words that describe this sculpture. State facts, not opinions.

Example: _rough_____

1. _____

2. _____

3. _____

4. _____

INTERPRETATION

Look at *Monekana* by Deborah Butterfield again. Pretend you own a real horse that has some of the same characteristics that the artist captures in her sculpture.

What would you call your horse?

_____

What sort of personality does it have?

Example: _excitable_____

_____

_____

Would you keep the horse wild or try to ride it? Why? If you want to ride it, where would you go?

_____

_____

Look at both *Cadeau* by Man Ray and *Swing* by Sam Gilliam on page 243. Write down three details about each artwork.

Cadeau

Example: *The iron has sharp tacks glued on its bottom.*

1. _____

2. _____

3. _____

Swing

4. _____

5. _____

6. _____

In what way are the two artworks similar?

_____

_____

_____

_____

In what way are the two artworks different?

_____

_____

_____

_____

Name _____ Date _____

Can we think with the heart?

READING 1: From *The Story of My Life*

VOCABULARY   **Key Words** *Use with textbook page 247.*

Write each word in the box next to its definition.

| bitterness | defects | eventful | imitate | sensation | tangible |

Example: ___*imitate*___: to copy the way someone else speaks, moves, etc.

1. _____: the ability to feel, or a feeling that you get from one of your five senses

2. _____: full of interesting or important events

3. _____: faults that make something not perfect

4. _____: anger because you feel that something happening to you is not fair

5. _____: clear enough or definite enough to be easily seen or noticed

Use the words in the box at the top of the page to complete the sentences.

6. Nino's baby sister likes to copy and _____ everything he does.

7. Ideas are not _____ because you cannot feel or touch them.

8. The tools are tested for _____ and problems before they are sold.

9. Because of her _____ toward others, she had a hard time getting along with other people.

10. Chris had a strange _____ in her elbow after she hit it on the door.

Read the paragraph below. Pay attention to the underlined academic words.

When I was younger, my sister and I built a tree house. First we came up with a <u>concept</u> for it. Then we got the wood and nails we would need. It took a good deal of <u>manual</u> labor to build the tree house. We were careful to <u>communicate</u> as we worked to put it together. With <u>persistence</u> and teamwork, we built a fine tree house.

Write the academic words from the paragraph above next to their correct definitions.

Example: <u>*communicate*</u> : express your thoughts and feelings so that other people understand them

1. _____ : the act of continuing firmly in some state, purpose, or course of action

2. _____ : having to do with the hand or hands

3. _____ : idea

Use the academic words from the paragraph above to complete the sentences.

4. It is important to _____ with people to explain your ideas and emotions.

5. We can understand the _____ of blood flowing through the body by studying a diagram of it.

6. The _____ alphabet uses fingers to spell words.

7. People with _____ do not give up and often overcome many hardships.

Complete the sentences with your own ideas.

Example: Jean showed his persistence by _*going for extra help every day after school*_.

8. My favorite way to communicate is _____.

9. In math, I learned the concept of _____.

10. Manual skills I use include _____.

Name _____ Date _____

> **REMEMBER** A suffix is a group of letters added to the end of a word that often changes the base word's part of speech and meaning. The suffix -ful means "full of." Adding the suffix -ful to a noun forms an adjective. When adding -ful to a word that has two or more syllables and ends in *y*, such as the word *beauty*, change the *y* to an *i* before adding -ful.

Look at the chart below. Form a new word by adding the suffix -ful to each base word. Write the new word on the chart. Then write the meaning.

Base Word	+ ful	Meaning
fear	fearful	*afraid, or full of fear*
1. health		
2. cheer		
3. peace		
4. pain		
5. success		

Add the suffix -ful to the nouns in parentheses. Then write sentences of your own with the new adjectives.

Example: (arm) __*armful*   *He was carrying an armful of groceries.*__

6. (skill) _____

7. (grace) _____

8. (bowl) _____

9. (taste) _____

10. (use) _____

11. (fright) _____

12. (cup) _____

13. (truth) _____

14. (hope) _____

15. (doubt) _____

Use with textbook page 249.

REMEMBER The main idea is the most important idea in one part of a text. Details are facts, examples, or other bits of information that support the main idea.

Read each paragraph and underline the main idea.

1. Have you ever heard this: "Everybody talks about the weather, but no one does anything about it"? We do talk about the weather a lot! We are fascinated by it. That's why weather reports on TV are so well watched.

2. To prepare their TV reports, weather reporters, many of whom are scientists, depend on sophisticated equipment. More than twelve weather satellites go around Earth. Other satellites sit about 22,000 miles above the equator. Their cameras photograph our entire planet.

Read each paragraph and circle the details.

3. The U.S. Fish and Wildlife Service protects many of America's birds, mammals, and fish. It helps save wetlands and protects endangered animals. The Service has 370 wildlife protection areas on 32 million acres in the U.S.

4. In Florida, the Wildlife Service protects many animals. The Service protects crocodiles, marsh snakes, and panthers. Every year, millions of people visit the Everglades and other wild areas in the state to see the wild animals. They know this is one of the few places they can see up close the animals the Wildlife Service protects.

Read the paragraph and underline the main idea. Then circle the details.

5. Humboldt squid are very large. They can grow to more than seven feet and weigh more than 100 pounds. For this reason they are commonly called "jumbo squid." Their growth rate is amazingly fast. In one year they can grow from the size of a grain of rice to the size of a human teenager.

COMPREHENSION   *Use with textbook page 256.*

Choose the best answer for each item. Circle the letter of the correct answer.

1. When Helen Keller lost her senses of sight and hearing, _____.

   a. she eventually got used to the silence

   b. she gave up and just sat in her room

   c. she blamed her parents

2. When Helen's aunt finally sewed the beads on Helen's doll, it meant that _____.

   a. Helen no longer wanted the doll

   b. she understood what Helen wanted

   c. she was going to take the doll away

3. In her writing, Helen often describes a scene _____.

   a. by drawing symbols

   b. by using what someone else said

   c. by using her senses of taste and smell

4. Anne Sullivan was not only Helen's teacher but also _____.

   a. her friend

   b. her aunt

   c. her nanny

5. What Anne Sullivan helped Helen to understand was that _____.

   a. she would never be able to communicate

   b. that her family loved her

   c. that finger motions symbolized words

EXTENSION   *Use with textbook page 257.*

In this story, Helen Keller relates important events from her life. Fill in the chart with important events from your life in chronological order.

Event #1	Event #2	Event #3	Event #4	Event #5

GRAMMAR

Possessive Adjectives *Use with textbook page 258.*

> **REMEMBER** A possessive adjective tells who owns something. It is always followed by a noun. It agrees with the noun or pronoun that reflects who the owner is. The possessive adjectives are *my, your, her, his, its, our,* and *their.* **Examples:** *my* book, *our* dog

Complete each sentence with the correct possessive adjective. Circle the word or words that the possessive adjective refers to.

my	your	her	his	its	our	their

Example: (Maria) loves _____ *her* _____ dog.

1. Pamela said that vanilla is _____ favorite ice cream flavor.

2. I used _____ own money to buy a new car.

3. You need to clean up _____ room.

4. My husband and I sold _____ house last year.

5. At the lake, each man had _____ own fishing gear.

Write sentences that show possession. Use the subjects in parentheses. Be sure to use the correct possessive adjective.

Example: (the dog) _*The dog sat in its dog house all day*_.

6. (Sarah and Tom) _____.

7. (I) _____.

8. (the woman) _____.

9. (they) _____.

10. (my father) _____.

WRITING

Write a Critique *Use with textbook page 259.*

This is the T-chart that Santos completed before writing his paragraph.

Standards met	Standards not met
exciting	
inspiring	
based on a true story	
uplifting	

Complete your own T-chart for a critique of a story, book, movie, or play.

Standards met	Standards not met

UNIT
4

Can we think with the heart?

READING 2: From *The Little Prince: The Play*

REMEMBER A **fantasy** is an imaginative story that includes characters, settings, or events not found in real life. **Stage directions** are instructions that tell the actors in a play what they should do and how they should do it.

Read each description and write whether it's an example of fantasy or stage directions.

Literary Word	Description
stage directions	[*He bends down and picks up a rusted lamp.*]
1.	[*Carl wanders off stage left in confusion.*]
2.	The mermaid reclined on a rock in the harbor.
3.	[*She walks from stage left to center stage.*]
4.	The goblin cast a spell on the princess in the castle.

Write examples of stage direction and fantasy in the chart below.

Literary Word	Description
stage direction	[*He gives the woman a hug.*]
5. stage direction	
6. fantasy	
7. stage direction	
8. fantasy	
9. stage direction	
10. fantasy	

Name _____ Date _____

VOCABULARY **Academic Words** *Use with textbook page 262.*

Read the paragraph below. Pay attention to the underlined academic words.

> *Wolf* is a modern <u>version</u> of a classic monster movie. In this movie, the people of a small town become curious about the <u>source</u> of the strange sounds they hear at night. They soon <u>establish</u> that some kind of wild animal is coming into the town. The villagers set a trap and discover a <u>unique</u> creature that is half human and half wolf.

Write the letter of the correct definition next to each word.

Example: ___c___ establish

a. the cause of something or the place where it starts

_____ **1.** source

b. a reworking of an existing work

_____ **2.** unique

c. begin or set in motion

_____ **3.** version

d. being the one and only one of its kind

Use the academic words from the exercise above to complete the sentences.

4. The comic is a new _____ of a story that was written five years ago.

5. The necklace is _____. It is one of a kind.

6. Nick plans to _____ a business in his home.

7. The heart is the _____ of blood moving around the body.

Complete the sentences with your own ideas.

Example: I think Luc is unique because *there is no one else like him in the world*.

8. The version of the story I like best _____.

9. The source of my happiness is _____.

10. I establish a friendship by _____.

REMEMBER A contraction is a word that comes from two words that have been joined. One or more letters are left out. An apostrophe is inserted where the letters have been deleted. For example, *do* and *not* can be joined to form the contraction *don't*.

Look at the chart below. Form the contraction for each pair of words. Write the contraction in the chart.

Word 1	Word 2	Contraction
could	not	*couldn't*
1. she	will	
2. you	have	
3. let	us	
4. they	are	
5. we	would	

Look at the chart below. Write the two words that form each contraction.

Contraction	Word 1	Word 2
I'm	*I*	*am*
6. you're		
7. she'd		
8. let's		
9. wouldn't		
10. it's		

Write a statement or question of your own for each of the contractions in the box.

they're	he's	let's	shouldn't	couldn't

11. _____   **14.** _____

12. _____   **15.** _____

13. _____

130

READING STRATEGY | ANALYZE TEXT STRUCTURE

Use with textbook page 263.

> **REMEMBER** Analyze text structure to find out what kind of text you are reading. Stories are written in paragraphs and the dialogue is enclosed within quotation marks. Poems are usually written in groups of lines. Plays are mostly written in dialogue and have stage directions in parentheses or brackets.

Read each text below and write whether it's from a story, a poem, or a play.

1. An ant fell on a leaf floating in a river. "Help! Help!" the ant yelled. A bird threw a small stick in the ant's direction.
   "Grab this!" the bird said to the ant. The ant grabbed the stick and got safely to the shore. The ant and the bird became friends for ever after.

   This text is a _____.

2. How beautiful is the rain!
   After the dust and heat,
   In the wide and dry street,
   How beautiful is the rain!

   This text is a _____.

3. **Nevaeh:** Is the book good?
   Lamar: [*looking up from reading*] It's great!

   This text is a _____.

4. The heat
   beats
   d
   o
   w
   n
   on the shimmering ground.

   This text is a _____.

5. We never had pets. "Not in an apartment," Mom said. I wanted an adorable pup. And then, one day, Mom said we could have a dog! I was so happy.

   This text is a _____.

Choose the best answer for each item. Circle the letter of the correct answer.

1. The fox is most afraid of _____.

   a. being tamed   **b.** men with guns   **c.** falling into lakes

2. The fox thinks the prince is looking for _____.

   a. other princes   **b.** his home   **c.** chickens

3. The prince says the rose tried to _____.

   a. stick him with a thorn   **b.** tame him   **c.** make him laugh

4. The Little Prince tames the fox by _____.

   a. circling him, then sitting   **b.** yelling at him to   **c.** giving him food
       near him in silence   be his friend

5. The fox helped the Little Prince to learn _____.

   a. how to hunt   **b.** to grow roses   **c.** to trust and love

RESPONSE TO LITERATURE *Use with textbook page 273.*

Find a part of the play that you liked very much. Draw a picture of the scene.

GRAMMAR

Present and Past Progressive *Use with textbook page 274.*

> **REMEMBER** Use the present progressive to describe an ongoing action that is happening now. It is formed by the present tense of the verb *be* + a verb ending in *-ing*.
> **Example:** I am going to the movies with Carlos.
> The present progressive + *always* is used to express a repeated action. The past progressive is used to describe an ongoing action that was in progress in the past. It is formed by using the past tense of the verb *be* (*was* or *were*) + a verb ending in *-ing*.
> **Example:** Tim was finishing his homework when his mom called him to dinner.

Complete each sentence with the present or past progressive using the *-ing* form of the verb in parentheses.

Example: (talk) She is _____*talking*_____ on the telephone with her best friend.

1. (call) The volunteers are _____ voters to ask for their support.

2. (yell) During the game, the coach was _____ at the players.

3. (sleep) She was _____ soundly until the alarm went off.

4. (try) My mother is always _____ to lose weight.

5. (use) The students were _____ their calculators during the exam.

Complete each sentence with the correct form of the verb *be* (*is, are, was, were*) plus the *-ing* form of the verb in parentheses.

Example: (wear) Maria _____*is wearing*_____ a beautiful dress tonight.

6. (take) At this time last year, we _____ exams.

7. (bake) Right now, my grandmother _____ her famous shrimp dish for our annual family dinner.

8. (fish) We had fun when we _____ last summer.

9. (give) The teacher _____ us a test now.

10. (invite) We _____ the whole neighborhood to tonight's party.

WRITING

Write a Summary *Use with textbook page 275.*

This is the word web that Adrian completed before writing his paragraph.

Main Idea
It's about a lonely prince and a fox who become friends.

Detail
He asks the fox if he'd like to play, but the fox is scared.

Detail
Every day he meets the fox and the fox gets used to him.

Detail
The fox teaches him "It is only with the heart that one can see rightly."

Complete your own main-idea-and-details word web summarizing a story, play, book, movie or television show.

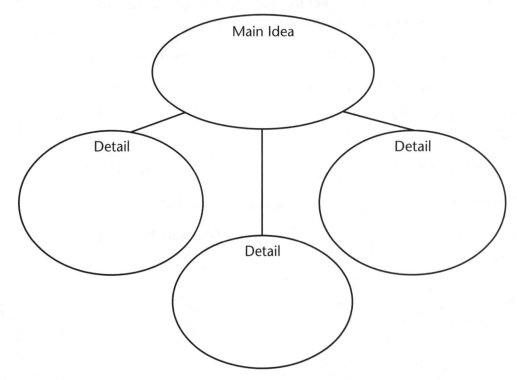

Main Idea

Detail

Detail

Detail

Name _____ Date _____

Can we think with the heart?

READING 3: "The Heart: Our Circulatory System" /
"Heart Healthy Recipe"

VOCABULARY **Key Words** *Use with textbook page 277.*

Write each word in the box next to its definition.

| arteries | blood vessels | capillaries | circulatory | pulmonary | veins |

Example: _____*circulatory*_____ : moving around within a system

1. _____ : very small, narrow tubes that carry blood
   around your body

2. _____ : the tubes through which blood flows to your
   heart from other parts of your body

3. _____ : relating to or affecting the lungs

4. _____ : the tubes that carry blood from your heart to
   the rest of your body

5. _____ : larger tubes through which blood flows in
   your body

Use the words in the box at the top of the page to complete the sentences below.

6. Special kinds of doctors study the _____ system, or how blood flows
   through your body.

7. It is necessary for blood to move through your _____ to your heart.

8. When your heart is beating faster, blood moving through the _____
   is pumped quicker to the rest of your body.

9. You cannot see your _____ under your skin because they are so tiny.

10. If you have asthma, you might want to see a doctor who specializes in

    _____ medicine.

Read the paragraph below. Pay attention to the underlined academic words.

> The heart pumps blood throughout the body <u>constantly</u>. Nerves connected to the heart <u>regulate</u> the speed at which the heart muscle tightens and relaxes. When the heart <u>contracts</u> it pushes blood to all parts of the body. A <u>network</u> of blood vessels can <u>transport</u> blood to each cell in the body.

Write academic words from the paragraph above next to their correct definitions.

Example: _____*network*_____ : a system of lines or tubes that cross one another and are connected to each other

1. _____: move or carry from one place to another

2. _____: become smaller or tighter

3. _____: always or regularly

4. _____: adjust things within a system to keep the system operating well

Use academic words from the paragraph above to complete the sentences.

5. All the blood vessels in our body are linked to form a _____.

6. Trucks _____ fruits and vegetables all across the United States.

7. Your heart works _____. It never stops!

8. Sweating is one way that the body can _____ and control heat.

Complete the sentences with your own ideas.

Example: The music is constantly on my mind *after hearing it at the concert last week* .

9. One way I can contract the muscles in my arm is to _____.

10. My parents often have to transport me to and from _____.

Name _____ Date _____

WORD STUDY   **Related Words**   *Use with textbook page 279.*

REMEMBER Related words are in the same word family. They are formed from the same base words and have related meanings. **Examples:** *analyze, analysis, analytical*
If you learn the meaning of one word in a word family, you can figure out the meanings of other words in that family.

Look at the chart below. Write the part of speech and meaning of each word.

Word	Part of Speech	Meaning
contradict	*verb*	*to disagree with*
contradiction	*noun*	*a disagreement*
1. regulate		
2. regulation		
3. muscle		
4. muscular		
5. reject		
6. rejection		

Write the part of speech and meaning for each word below. Then use each word in a sentence of your own. Use a dictionary if necessary.

Example: digest   *to process food so that it can be absorbed by the body*
     Some foods are easier to digest than others.

     digestion   *the process or ability to break down food*
     Digestion begins in the mouth when you chew food.

7. transport _____

_____

8. transportation _____

_____

9. microscope _____

_____

10. microscopic _____

_____

Unit 4 • Reading 3   **137**

Use with textbook page 279.

REMEMBER Monitoring comprehension is a way to help you understand a text. As you read, stop to ask yourself how much you have understood. Reread the text and try to understand new words and ideas. Try to put the information in the text into your own words.

Read the paragraph. Then answer the questions that follow.

The lungs are spongy, filled with hundreds of millions of tiny air-filled sacs called alveoli. Each air sac is surrounded by capillaries. Oxygen that has been breathed into the lungs passes through the walls of the sacs and into the capillaries, where it binds to the hemoglobin in the blood. Carbon dioxide escapes from the blood into the alveoli and is exhaled. The blood returns to the left atrium by way of the pulmonary veins.

1. Read the paragraph again and underline phrases or words that are hard to understand.

2. Reread the lines with difficult words or phrases. Write your best guess about what these words and phrases mean.

   _____

   _____

3. Use a dictionary to check the meanings of words or phrases you're not sure about. Write their meanings in your own words.

   _____

   _____

4. What is the passage about?

   _____

   _____

5. How does the skill of monitoring comprehension help you understand what you read?

   _____

   _____

COMPREHENSION   *Use with textbook page 286.*

Choose the best answer for each item. Circle the letter of the correct answer.

1. Your heart is about the size of _____.

   a. your eye   **b.** your head   **c.** your fist

2. Your heart weighs about as much as a _____.

   a. big bag of rice   **b.** sneaker   **c.** strawberry

3. Plasma is a _____.

   a. liquid   **b.** type of heart muscle   **c.** type of blood tube

4. The most common cells in the human body are _____.

   a. white blood cells   **b.** clear blood cells   **c.** red blood cells

5. Blood flows _____.

   a. at the same rate   **b.** faster from the heart   **c.** slower from the heart
      throughout the body

EXTENSION   *Use with textbook page 287.*

Read the heart-healthy recipe on page 285. Think of another recipe that you like that uses healthy ingredients. Write it here and share it with the class.

_____

_____

_____

_____

_____

_____

_____

_____

_____

Imperatives *Use with textbook page 288.*

> **REMEMBER** Imperatives are used to give directions, orders, advice or warnings. The implied subject is always *you* but you do not write it. **Example:** Watch out!
> Imperatives are also used to make requests and invitations. Use the word *please* with those imperatives. The negative form is usually expressed by *Don't*.

Circle the imperative verb or verbs in each pair of sentences.

1. Answer the telephone. It's been ringing for a long time.

2. Don't forget to water the plants. It's important!

3. It's snowing outside. Come in, please.

4. See a specialist about your leg. It looks as though it's broken.

5. You are too kind. Stop sending me presents.

Complete each sentence with a word from the box. After each sentence, write whether the imperative conveys directions, advice, a warning, a request, or an invitation.

come	take	stop	join	remember	open

Example: _____*Open*_____ the door! Your mother will be angry. ____*warning*____

6. Please _____ to our house for dinner. _____

7. _____ smoking! _____

8. _____ to put on mosquito protection. _____

9. _____ the next right at the stop light. _____

10. Please _____ me in singing "Happy Birthday!" _____

WRITING

Write Instructions *Use with textbook page 289.*

This is the graphic organizer that Evan completed before writing his paragraph.

1. Get a blender and plug it into an outlet.

↓

2. Decide which types of fruits you are going to have.

↓

3. If you are using fruits that have a peel, take the peel off.

↓

4. Mix all of the fruits in the blender.

↓

5. Drink and enjoy!

Complete your own graphic organizer giving step-by-step instructions about how to do something.

1.

↓

2.

↓

3.

↓

4.

↓

5.

UNIT
4

Can we think with the heart?

READING 4: "Ginger for the Heart"

VOCABULARY **Literary Words** *Use with textbook page 291.*

REMEMBER A **symbol** is anything that stands for or represents something else.

Label each phrase with what it represents.

Symbol	What does it stand for?
smiley face	*happiness*
flag at half mast	1.
thumbs up	2.
snail	3.

Read the stanza below the poem "Uphill" by Christina Rossetti. Think about what it means. Then answer the questions that follow.

> Does the road wind uphill all the way?
> Yes, to the very end.
> Will the day's journey take the whole long day?
> From morn to night, my friend.

Example: What is the "day's journey" a symbol for? _____*life*_____

4. What do morn and night represent? _____

5. Why is the journey uphill? _____

Copyright © by Pearson Education, Inc.

142   **Unit 4 • Reading 4**

VOCABULARY **Academic Words** *Use with textbook page 292.*

Read the paragraph below. Pay attention to the underlined academic words.

> Love is such an <u>abstract</u> idea in the English language that it is difficult to define. The word love can be used to refer to the <u>mutual</u> affection between two people in a romantic relationship. It can also describe the feelings of a person <u>devoted</u> to family or friends. Love can have a more general meaning, as in a love of life or humanity. However love is defined, there is no denying its <u>significance</u>.

Write the letter of the correct definition next to each word.

Example: ___*b*___ abstract

_____ 1. devoted

_____ 2. mutual

_____ 3. significance

a. importance or meaning of something

b. existing only as an idea or quality rather than as something concrete you can see and touch

c. felt by two or more people toward one another

d. giving someone or something a lot of love, concern, or attention

Use the academic words from the exercise above to complete the sentences.

4. Julio and Maria had a _____ interest in music so they formed a band.

5. Wisdom is an _____ term because it is a quality you cannot see or touch.

6. The book has great _____ for me because it was a gift from her father.

7. The cat is _____ to her kittens and takes good care of them.

Complete the sentences with your own ideas.

Example: A heart is often an abstract symbol for _____*love*_____.

8. Because of our mutual respect, my friends and I _____.

9. The person I am devoted to the most is _____.

10. A gift I once received had great significance to me because _____

_____

REMEMBER The /z/ sound can be spelled with the letters *z, x,* and *s.* The letter that most often stands for the /z/ sound is the letter *s.* The /z/ sound can come at the beginning or end of a syllable.
Examples: *zest, blizzard, xylophone, examine, boys, amuse, she's, because*

Say each word to yourself. Circle the word in each pair that contains the /z/ sound.

Example: sad, (zap)

1. sip, unzip

2. hippos, hippopotamus

3. this, these

4. stream, streams

5. zealous, seal

6. hazy, haste

7. as, so

8. example, explain

Rewrite the sentences below by replacing the underlined words with a word from the box.

~~zombies~~	busy	houses	maze	exact	survives	zone	stories

Example: Many scary movies feature <u>the walking dead</u>.

Many scary movies feature zombies.

9. The hero of this story <u>doesn't die</u>.

_____

10. The construction <u>area</u> is dangerous.

_____

11. My mother used to read me great <u>tales</u> at night.

_____

12. These <u>homes</u> need repair.

_____

13. It's easy to get lost in a <u>labyrinth</u>.

_____

14. I am <u>always working</u>.

_____

15. As a scientist, you have to be <u>precise</u>.

_____

READING STRATEGY | ANALYZE CULTURAL CONTEXT

Use with textbook page 293.

> **REMEMBER** Analyzing the cultural context (the beliefs, art, ideas of a particular group) of a story helps you understand it better.

Read the passage and answer the questions that follow.

Buddhism has many followers. It is one of the largest religions in the world. Narayan is a Buddhist. He lives in Tibet. He wants to study to become a monk. He wants to travel to India to visit the Dalai Lama. The Dalai Lama is one of a long line of Dalai Lamas that traces back to 1391. Ever since he was little, Narayan has known that "Dalai" means "Ocean" in Mongolian, while "Lama" is the Tibetan word for "guru," or "spiritual teacher."

1. What words or phrases in the passage above are new to you?

   _____

   _____

2. Look up the word "Tibet" in an encyclopedia or on the Internet. Where is Tibet?

   _____

   _____

3. Look up "Dalai Lama" in an encylopedia or on the Internet. Write one fact that you learned about the Dalai Lama.

   _____

   _____

4. Why do you think Narayan wants to visit the Dalai Lama?

   _____

   _____

5. How can analyzing the cultural context help you better understand this passage?

   _____

   _____

Choose the best answer for each item. Circle the letter of the correct answer.

1. Yenna and her mother work _____.

    a. sewing   **b.** in the gold fields   **c.** cooking in a castle

2. Yenna gives the young man a ginger root _____.

    a. because he is sick   **b.** to remind him of her   **c.** to protect him
                                       and her love

3. The young man returns after going away to _____.

    a. find his parents   **b.** clear his debt   **c.** return to China

4. The flame Yenna lights in her window symbolizes _____.

    a. her constant love for   **b.** how long she sews   **c.** the color of the sun
        the young man

5. When the ginger root does not burn in the fire, it means _____.

    a. they will never die   **b.** the young man will   **c.** their love can endure
                                          go away forever   anything

RESPONSE TO LITERATURE   *Use with textbook page 299.*

Imagine that the young man did not come back for Yenna. What do you think would happen then? Write a new ending for the story.

_____

_____

_____

_____

_____

GRAMMAR

Compound and Complex Sentences *Use with textbook page 300.*

> **REMEMBER** A compound sentence contains two independent clauses. They are usually connected with coordinating conjunctions such as *and, but, or,* or *so.*
> **Example:** We will go to the zoo tomorrow, and Dad will meet us after for dinner.
> A complex sentence contains an independent clause and a dependent clause, which are connected with a subordinating conjunction, such as *while, though, because,* or *until.*
> **Example:** Let's keep playing until it gets dark.

Write whether the sentence is a compound sentence or a complex sentence. Underline the coordinating or subordinating conjunctions in each sentence. In the space at the end of the sentence write *cc* or *sc* to specify the type of conjunction.

Example: _compound sentence_ Many buildings are made from brick, <u>but</u> these are made out of concrete. __cc__

1. _____ He was a very skinny boy until he began exercising. _____

2. _____ I go to school every day, and then I go to the gym. _____

3. _____ He finally finished the project, or so he led me to believe. _____

Combine the two sentences with the conjunction in parentheses.

Example: She wanted to become a dancer. She broke her foot. (*but*)

She wanted to become a dancer, but she broke her foot.

4. They lived in an apartment. Then they bought a house. (*until*)

_____

5. The old woman fed the baby. The mother rested. (*while*)

_____

WRITING

Write a Critical Analysis *Use with textbook page 301.*

This is the T-chart that Andrea completed before writing her paragraph.

Ideas	Textual evidence
The ginger root symbolizes the couple's enduring love. Like their love, it was too strong to be destroyed.	The ginger root stayed "firm and fragrant" for four years. The man's sweat and tears kept it moist. The ginger root didn't burn when he threw it into the fire.

Complete your own T-chart for a critical analysis of a story or another piece of literature.

Ideas	Textual evidence

148

Unit 4 • Reading 4

Can we think with the heart?

UNIT 4

READING 5: "To Capture the Wild Horse"

VOCABULARY **Root Words and Cognates** *Use with textbook pages 303–304.*

Determine the meaning of the underlined word in each sentence below. Use cognates, your knowledge of Greek and Latin roots, and any context clues to figure out the meaning. Write your definition on the first line. Then look up the word in a dictionary and write the dictionary definition on the second line. See how close you came.

1. Many colors are <u>visible</u> to insects but cannot be seen by humans.

_____

_____

2. Hayden Herrera wrote a very interesting <u>biography</u> of painter Frida Kahlo.

_____

_____

3. People can make calls nearly anywhere now that telephones are completely <u>portable</u>.

_____

_____

4. We are going to <u>dissect</u> a worm in science class today.

_____

_____

5. A <u>transatlantic</u> telegraph cable allowed Americans to communicate with Europeans in a few minutes, rather than ten days.

_____

_____

6. The sisters were <u>reunited</u> after many years of separation.

_____

_____

Elements of Drama

Use with textbook pages 305–306.

> **REMEMBER** A **dramatic convention** is a kind of agreement between the people who create a play and the audience that watches it. Often these conventions help the audience understand the characters and plot. Sometimes they make the play entertaining or intense for the audience, too. Some examples of dramatic conventions are the fourth wall, a narrator, character asides, dramatic irony, and soliloquies.

Read the following excerpt from a play. The setting is the early 1900s. Then fill out the graphic organizer below it.

Mayor: *[To the audience]* My name is Mayor George Hotshot, and this is my town. See that big building in the town square? That's city hall. My office is in there. That's where I decide all my big . . . well, decisions. Do you see that woman coming around the corner? That's Marisol Perez. She's the newspaper editor. She never likes any of my decisions. *[To Marisol]* Good morning, Marisol.

Marisol: Good morning, George. What damage have you done this morning?

Mayor: You always like your little joke, don't you, Marisol?

Marisol: Who's joking? I heard you're trying to outlaw automobiles in town.

Mayor: You bet I am. They scare the horses. And they're just a fad. The automobile won't last more than a year. Mark my words.

Marisol: I always do, George. Then I write the opposite in my paper. It gives me a great reputation for being right.

Mayor: *[Laughing]* Always the comedian. *[He goes to sit at his desk.]*

Marisol: *[To herself]* If only I could get Mr. Hotshot out of the mayor's office, this town could be successful. I think it's time to do some investigating.

Question	Identify	Effect on Play
Who is the narrator?		
How does the play use dramatic irony?		
Who gives a soliloquy, and why?		

LITERARY ANALYSIS **Literary Tradition** *Use with textbook pages 307–308.*

> **REMEMBER** Playwrights use themes, stories, characters, and images from literature of the past. Reusing myths, tales, and other literature can add interest and help readers see modern themes and situations in new ways.

Here is an example of a classical narrative poem and a twenty-first-century play based on it. Read the two summaries and answer the questions below.

Ovid's narrative poem *Metamorphoses* (8 C.E.): "Orpheus and Eurydice"	Sarah Ruhl's play *Eurydice* (2006)
Orpheus and Eurydice are married and in love. One day she steps on a snake and dies. Orpheus is extremely upset. He goes to the underworld and begs Hades to bring Eurydice back to life. He constantly plays sweet songs on his lyre to persuade Hades. Hades finally agrees, but gives Orpheus one condition: as Orpheus leads Eurydice out of the underworld, he cannot look back to check on her, not even once. But Orpheus gives in to temptation and looks back at Eurydice. So Eurydice falls back in to the underworld forever.	On the day of Eurydice and Orpheus's wedding, Eurydice is visited by a man who says he has a letter from Eurydice's father, who is dead. She follows the man to his apartment, but ends up falling to her death. She enters the underworld, where she encounters her father. Orpheus sends her love letters, trying to get her back. But Eurydice cannot decide whether she wants to return to her husband or stay with her father. She finally decides to stay with her father. So she calls out to Orpheus when he tries to retrieve her, causing him to look back at her. Eurydice stays in the underworld with her father.

1. How are these two stories alike? How are they different?

   _____

   _____

   _____

2. How has Ruhl changed the theme, or message, of Ovid's story?

   _____

   _____

   _____

LITERARY ANALYSIS

Here is an example of an ancient Greek play and a twentieth-century American play based on it. Read the two summaries and answer the questions below.

Ancient Greek play: *The Oresteia* by Aeschylus	Twentieth-century American play: *Mourning Becomes Electra* by Eugene O'Neill
Agamemnon, the King of Argos, is returning home from the Trojan War. During the war, Agamemnon sacrificed his daughter Iphigenia in order to get the Greek ships to sail. (He had offended a goddess and needed to please her.) His wife, Clytemnestra, is furious and plans to seek revenge. She ends Agamemnon's life when he returns. Later, at Agamemnon's gravesite, another daughter, Electra, meets her younger brother Orestes. She hasn't seen him in many years. They discuss their father's death. Together, they seek revenge against their mother and her new husband, Aegisthus. Orestes kills them both. But the "Erinyes"—angry deities—are angry with Orestes for killing his own mother. The angry Erinyes haunt Orestes.	General Ezra Mannon fought in the American Civil War, which has just ended. He is returning home, but his wife Christine detests him. With her friend Adam Brant, she plans to poison Ezra after his return. Christine and Ezra have two children—Orin and Lavinia. One day Lavinia finds Ezra just after Christine poisons him. After Ezra's death, he haunts his family and home. Lavinia is furious with her mother about her father's being poisoned. Christine also despises Lavinia but adores Orin. This makes Lavinia very jealous. When Orin realizes that Christine poisoned Ezra in order to spend more time with Adam, he and Lavinia decide to end Adam's life in revenge. This event also brings about the end of Christine's life.

1. How can you tell that O'Neill's play is based on *The Oresteia*? Consider the names, the plot, and the situations of the main characters.

_____

_____

2. Based on the summaries, how do the two plays seem different?

_____

_____

LITERARY ANALYSIS   **How Genre Shapes Meaning**
Use with textbook page 309.

Here is a fable by Aesop and a scene from a play based on it. Read the selections below and then answer the questions.

"The Fox and the Grapes"

One hot summer's day a Fox was strolling through an orchard till he came to a bunch of Grapes just ripening on a vine which had been trained over a lofty branch. "Just the thing to quench my thirst," quoth he. Drawing back a few paces, he took a run and a jump, and just missed the bunch. Turning round again with a One, Two, Three, he jumped up, but with no greater success. Again and again he tried after the tempting morsel, but at last had to give it up, and walked away with his nose in the air, saying: "I am sure they are sour."

Scene from a play based on "The Fox and the Grapes"

[*In a noisy high school cafeteria*]
Carmen: [*eating a sandwich*] Hey, Amy, did you make the choir? Didn't the list get posted this morning?
[*Amy says nothing, stares at the floor*]
Ricardo: Yeah, what happened, Amy? We know how hard you've been practicing.
Amy: Um, actually, I don't think I was practicing *that* hard.
Ricardo: You were totally practicing. You practiced that recital song over and over!
Amy: Shut up, Ricardo. My name wasn't on the list.
Carmen: Oh, no! I'm really sorry.
Amy: Well, it's not like I care. Besides, choir is really stupid.

---

1. What do the fable and the play have in common?

   _____

   _____

2. Do you interpret each version in the exact same way? Or do the genres affect the meaning? Explain your answer.

   _____

   _____

Nominative, Objective, and Possessive Pronouns *Use with textbook page 313.*

REMEMBER Pronouns are words that replace nouns. They have different cases for different uses. A **nominative pronoun** is the subject of a sentence or clause. An **objective pronoun** is the direct object, the indirect object, or the object of a preposition. A **possessive pronoun** shows ownership.

Choose the correct pronoun from the parentheses to complete each sentence. Look at the chart on textbook page 313 for help.

1. The CD player lost (its, it's) cord.

   _____

2. Lisa left (she, her) books on the shelf.

   _____

3. Have you seen (me, my) jewelry box?

   _____

4. (She, Her) weaves very beautiful baskets.

   _____

5. Turn off the light when (you, your) leave the room.

   _____

6. Is that (his, him) jacket hanging on the doorknob?

   _____

7. (Her, Hers) paintings are always colorful.

   _____

8. The lamp fell off (its, it's) shelf.

   _____

9. Stand between John and (me, I).

   _____

WRITING **Write a Script** *Use with textbook pages 314–316.*

> **REMEMBER** A **script** can be about any topic. It usually involves two or more characters. Their talking, or dialogue, reveals their personalities and their situation. Scripts also have themes, or messages. Themes can be implicit (not stated directly) or explicit (stated directly). Scripts have a mood and tone. Writers create mood by using imagery to describe settings, objects, or emotions. Tone is a writer's attitude toward his or her subject.

To develop your ideas for your script, answer the questions below.

Who are the characters, or people?

_____

_____

_____

What is the situation, and what happens to the characters?

_____

_____

_____

How do they feel about what happens to them? (mood)

_____

_____

_____

What is my attitude toward the characters and situation? (tone)

_____

_____

_____

What lesson does the audience learn? (theme)

_____

_____

_____

Once you have decided what your play will be about, you can begin to organize your script. Fill in the flowchart below, summarizing what will happen in each scene of your script.

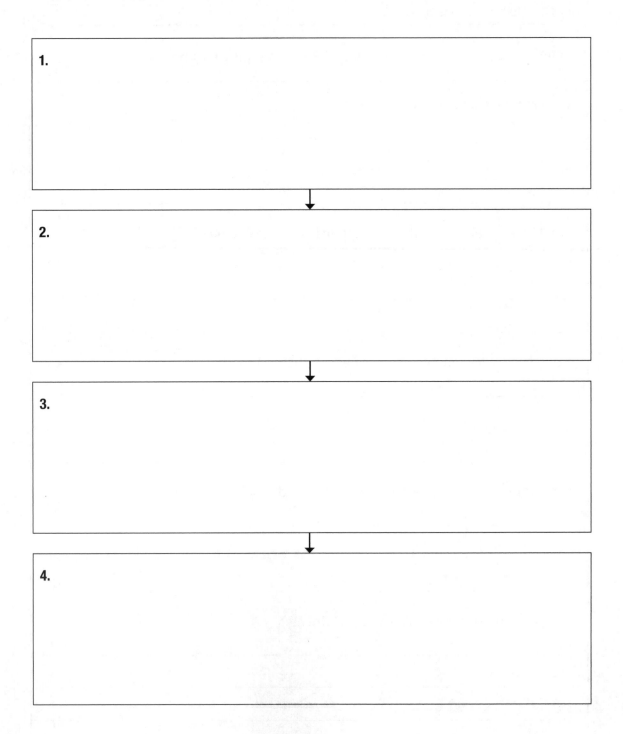

1.

2.

3.

4.

EDIT AND PROOFREAD *Use with textbook page 324.*

Read the paragraph below carefully. Look for mistakes in spelling, punctuation, and grammar. Correct the mistakes with the editing marks on Student Book page 553. Then rewrite the paragraph correctly on the lines below.

my school wanted to help our town. This time we wanted to do something speshul. We thought that about ten kids mite help, but sixty kids came to our meeting! we talked about what kinds of things we could do. Some kids wanted to recykle cans and bottils. Other kids wanted to clean the park. we decided to make a painting for the town hall. We were carefull not to spill paint. The painting was pretty. it was nice to see that peepil liked it sew much. We all painted our names on the bottom. I felt very proud.

_____

_____

_____

_____

_____

_____

_____

_____

Underline the vocabulary items you know and can use well. Review and practice any you haven't underlined. Underline them when you know them well.

Literary Words	Key Words		Academic Words	
fantasy	bitterness	arteries	communicate	constantly
stage directions	defects	blood vessels	concept	contract
symbol	eventful	capillaries	manual	network
	imitate	circulatory	persistence	regulate
	sensation	pulmonary	establish	transport
	tangible	veins	source	abstract
			unique	devoted
			version	mutual
				significance

Put a check by the skills you can perform well. Review and practice any you haven't checked off. Check them off when you can perform them well.

Skills	I can . . .
Word Study	☐ recognize and spell words with the suffix -ful. ☐ recognize and spell contractions. ☐ recognize and spell related words. ☐ recognize and spell words with the /z/ sound. ☐ recognize and use root words and cognates.
Reading Strategies	☐ identify main idea and details. ☐ analyze text structure. ☐ monitor comprehension. ☐ analyze cultural context.
Grammar	☐ use possessive adjectives. ☐ use the present and past progressive. ☐ use imperatives. ☐ use compound and complex sentences. ☐ use nominative, objective, and possessive pronouns.
Writing	☐ write a critique. ☐ write a summary. ☐ write instructions. ☐ write a critical analysis. ☐ write a script. ☐ write an expository essay.

Visual Literacy: Smithsonian American
Art Museum *Use with textbook pages 326–327.*

INTERPRETATION

Look at *Love Poem—Poem by Michael Hannon* by William T. Wiley on page 326. Why do you think Wiley placed the sailboat where he did? Where would you place it? Why?

_____

_____

_____

_____

_____

_____

COMPARE & CONTRAST

Look at *Hermia and Helena* by Washington Allston on page 327 and *Love Poem—Poem by Michael Hannon* by William T. Wiley again. Write down four similarities you see in the two works of art.

Similarities

1. _____

2. _____

3. _____

4. _____

Write down four differences you see in the two works of art.

Differences

1. _____

2. _____

3. _____

4. _____

Look at *Hermia and Helena* by Washington Allston again. Use the painting to complete the web diagram below. For each "string" coming from the center list one observation about the artwork. State facts, not opinions.

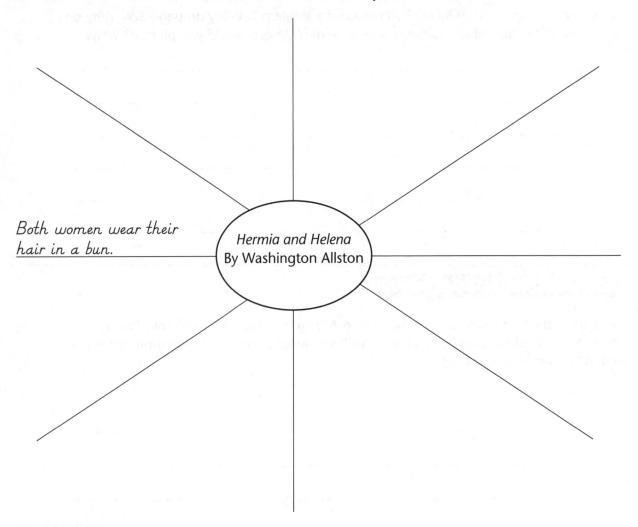

Both women wear their hair in a bun.

Hermia and Helena
By Washington Allston

MEDIA LITERACY

Now that you have read about matters of the heart, go to www.LongmanKeystone .com for links to the Smithsonian website. Follow the online instructions to compare the artwork in your student book with other media that convey similar messages. Which messages are conveyed more directly through visual media? Which ideas are conveyed more effectively through print or audio?

UNIT 5

What can we learn from times of war?

READING 1: "World War I"

VOCABULARY **Key Words** *Use with textbook page 331.*

Write each word in the box next to its definition.

| alliance | armistice | assassination | civilians | surrendered | trenches |

Example: ___*armistice*___: an agreement to stop fighting, usually for a specific period of time

1. _____: long narrow holes dug along the ground

2. _____: the murder of an important person

3. _____: a close agreement or connection between people, countries, etc.

4. _____: those who are not members of the military or the police

5. _____: an agreement to stop fighting

Use the words in the box at the top of the page to complete the sentences.

6. Do you think the _____ will last and there will be peace?

7. The thieves _____ to the police because they knew they were caught.

8. The _____ are muddy because the holes have filled with rain.

9. The king's _____ resulted in his son taking the throne.

10. An _____ joined together six countries.

Read the paragraph below. Pay attention to the underlined academic words.

When World War II began, the United States was <u>neutral</u>. Because of the <u>tension</u> that developed between Japan and the United States, Japan attacked Hawaii and America entered the war. America put much of its <u>resources</u> into fighting the war. Largely because of this, <u>technology</u> developed rapidly. In addition to improvements to <u>vehicles</u> such as tanks, advances were also made in aircraft and warships.

Write the academic words from the paragraph above next to their correct definition.

Example: ___*resources*___ : all the money, property, skills, and other goods that are available for use

1. _____ : machines such as cars, buses, or trucks used for carrying people or things from one place to another

2. _____ : not supporting either side in an argument, competition, or war

3. _____ : the combination of all the latest knowledge, equipment, and methods used in scientific or industrial work

4. _____ : the emotionally charged relationship between people or groups of people

Use the academic words from the paragraph above to complete the sentences.

5. The _____ between the two friends made everyone feel stressed.

6. The country had many _____, such as wood, diamonds, and gold.

7. Bicycles are the only _____ that kids under 16 can drive.

8. In World War I, the fighter plane was an example of new _____.

Complete the sentences with your own ideas.

Example: My brother can drive these vehicles: _*cars, buses, and motorcycles*_.

9. When friends fight, I remain neutral because _____.

10. One thing that causes tension in my life is _____.

Name _____ Date _____

REMEMBER Many English words contain Greek or Latin roots, or word parts. Knowing the meanings of common roots can help you figure out the meanings of unfamiliar words. For example, the English word *belligerent* contains the Latin root *bellum*, which means "war." A belligerent person is someone who is aggressive or warlike.

Look at the chart below. Notice the relationships between the roots, their meanings, and the English words that contain them. Then add a word from the box to the correct row on the chart.

tendon	photosynthesis	civilization	telescope	marine
centipede	portable	facsimile	technique	~~captain~~

Root	Meaning	Origin	English word
capit	head	Latin	capital *captain*
cent	one hundred	Latin	cent **1.**_____
civ	citizen	Latin	civil **2.**_____
fac	do, make	Latin	factor **3.**_____
mar	sea	Latin	marina **4.**_____
photo	light	Greek	photocopy **5.**_____
port	carry	Latin	import **6.**_____
scope	see, watch	Greek	stethoscope **7.**_____
techn	art, skill	Greek	hi-tech **8.**_____
tens	stretch, strain	Latin	tense **9.**_____

Use with textbook page 333.

> **REMEMBER** Identifying cause and effect can help you to understand a story's structure. The cause is why something happens in a story. The effect is what happens. Look for the words *so* and *because* to help you find cause and effect.

Read each paragraph. Underline the words that help you identify cause and effect.

1. The invention of air conditioners has greatly affected where people live. Cities like Phoenix, Atlanta, Dallas, and Houston grew because air conditioning made it possible to survive there during hot months. Today, many people can live in these places comfortably.

2. Maria went to a ranch to ride a horse. She had never been on a horse before, so the trainer led the horse.

Read each paragraph and find the cause and effect. Write them on the lines.

3. Oranges grow best during warm sunny days. Because the weather has been so cold this winter, the orange crop is damaged.

   Cause: _____

   Effect: _____

4. In the summer of 1993, huge amounts of rain fell on the Midwest. At times, as much as one inch of rain fell every six minutes. The rainstorms were caused by a warm current of water called El Niño.

   Cause: _____

   Effect: _____

5. How does the skill of identifying cause and effect help you to understand what you read?

   _____

   _____

Name _____ Date _____

Use with textbook page 340.

Circle the letter of the correct answer.

1. The word that best describes the feeling between the countries in Europe around

   1900 is _____.

   a. friendly   **b.** tense   **c.** neutral

2. The two countries in Europe that had an alliance with Britain were _____.

   a. Japan and China   **b.** Italy and Germany   **c.** France and Russia

3. Archduke Ferdinand was assassinated because _____.

   a. he declared war   **b.** the Serbians were angry   **c.** because he was king
       on Serbia   that Austria-Hungary   of Austria-Hungary
                                     controlled Bosnia
                                     and Herzegovina

4. One way new technology affected the fighting of WW I was that _____.

   a. inventors were given   **b.** new medicines were given   **c.** weapons became
       more money to   on the battlefield   deadlier
       make new machines
       for warfare

5. The United States entered World War I mainly because _____.

   a. the Germans sank   **b.** everyone in the United   **c.** the Japanese attacked
       United States ships   States supported   Pearl Harbor
                                     going to war

EXTENSION *Use with textbook page 341.*

**Imagine you were living in the United States during the beginning of World War I.
What do you suppose life would be like? How would you feel about the United
States entering World War I? Write your response below.**

_____

_____

_____

_____

_____

Appositives *Use with textbook page 342.*

> **REMEMBER** An appositive is a noun or noun phrase. It describes the noun that immediately precedes it.
> **Example:** The boy *who lives next door* mowed the grass between our lawns.
> A restrictive appositive contains information that is crucial to the sense of the sentence.
> **Example:** The house *which I bought* just burst into flames.
> A nonrestrictive appositive contains information that can be omitted without affecting the sense of the sentence. Use commas only with nonrestrictive appositives.
> **Example:** My only brother, *Jim*, is always teasing me.

Circle the appositive in each sentence below. On the line, write *R* if it is a restrictive appositive and *NR* if it is nonrestrictive.

Example: The assassination of Archduke Franz Ferdinand, ⟨heir to the throne of Austria-Hungary⟩ started World War I. _NR_

1. World War I, the first modern war, began in 1914. _____

2. Led by Woodrow Wilson, the U.S. president, the United States joined the war in 1917. _____

3. The United States had no choice but to declare war, because Germany had sunk some U.S. ships. _____

Combine each set of sentences below by using an appositive.

Example: Archduke Franz Ferdinand was shot in Sarajevo. Sarajevo is the capital of Serbia.
   Archduke Franz Ferdinand was shot in Sarajevo, the capital of Serbia.

4. The assassin was a Bosnian student. He was supported by Serbian terrorists.

   _____

5. Austria-Hungary declared war on Serbia. Austria-Hungary was the country Archduke Franz Ferdinand was to lead.

   _____

WRITING

Write a Cause-and-Effect Paragraph *Use with textbook page 343.*

This is the graphic organizer that Andrea completed before writing her news article.

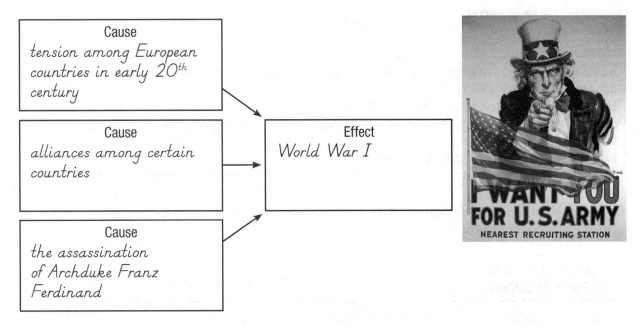

Cause
tension among European countries in early 20ᵗʰ century

Cause
alliances among certain countries

Cause
the assassination of Archduke Franz Ferdinand

Effect
World War I

Complete your own graphic organizer about a problem in your community, a conflict between social groups at your school, or a problem you learned about in social studies.

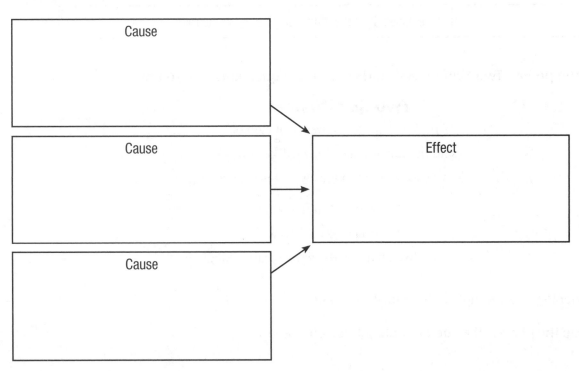

Cause

Cause

Cause

Effect

What can we learn from times of war?

READING 2: "In Flanders Fields" / "Anthem for Doomed Youth" / "Three Wonderful Letters from Home" / "Letter Home"

VOCABULARY   **Literary Words** *Use with textbook page 345.*

REMEMBER **Figurative language** describes one thing in terms of another. It will often appeal to the five senses to produce sensory effects.
Example: The birds' song was a *symphony* that started the girl's day.
One type of figurative language is personification. **Personification** gives human qualities to nonhuman things.
Example: The wind *whistled* through the trees.

Each sentence below uses figurative language. Label each one as an example of sensory effects or personification.

Sensory Effects or Personification	Sentence
personification	The table groaned with the weight of the books.
1.	The clouds looked like fluffy balls of cotton.
2.	The yellow tulips danced in the wind.
3.	Like rubies, the little tomatoes glittered in the rain.

Read the poem "Two Sunflowers" and answer the questions that follow.

Two Sunflowers

"Ah, William, we are weary of clouds,"

said the sunflowers, shining like lamps.

"Give us a room with a view!" they begged.

The sunflowers sat in the window.

Like princes on a throne

And they lived happily the whole season long!

4. Underline one example of figurative language.

5. Circle the phrases that are examples of personification.

VOCABULARY   **Academic Words** *Use with textbook page 346.*

Read the paragraph below. Pay attention to the underlined academic words.

> In this unit you'll read two poems about the <u>impact</u> of war and the death of soldiers. In order to appreciate these poems, you'll need to know about World War I. Understanding the <u>context</u> in which the poems were written will help you better understand them. Though the poems are <u>similar</u> in some ways, they <u>create</u> different views of war and dying.

Write the letter of the correct definition next to each word.

Example: __*c*__ context

_____ 1. create

_____ 2. impact

_____ 3. similar

a. make

b. almost the same

c. situation and conditions which surround something

d. the effect that an event or situation has on someone or something

Use the academic words from the exercise above to complete the sentences.

4. An accident can _____ a bad situation during rush hour.

5. The brother and sister are _____ but not exactly alike.

6. The lack of rain had a bad _____ on the crops.

7. Knowing the _____ of a novel will help the students understand it better.

Complete the sentences with your own ideas.

Example: My aunt is similar to _*my mother because they are sisters*_.

8. Understanding the context of a story I am reading helps me

_____.

9. With art materials, I like to create _____.

10. Whether or not I am getting along with my friends has a big impact on

_____.

REMEMBER A homophone is a word that sounds the same as another word but has a different meaning and spelling. For example, *knew* and *new* are homophones. *Knew* is a verb that means "understood"; *new* is an adjective that means "original or fresh."

Write your own definitions for each pair of homophones in the chart. Then check your definitions in a dictionary.

Homophones	Definitions
cells, sells	*the smallest living things; to exchange for money*
1. piece, peace	
2. your, you're	
3. waste, waist	
4. whole, hole	
5. course, coarse	

Write definitions for each pair of homophones. Then use both words in sentences. You can write a sentence for each word or use both words in one sentence.

Example: deer, dear ___*a large, wild animal; much loved*___

___*My dear mother admires deer.*___

6. board, bored _____

_____

7. bare, bear _____

_____

8. complement, compliment _____

_____

9. days, daze _____

_____

10. sight, site _____

_____

Name _____ Date _____

READING STRATEGY | ANALYZE HISTORICAL CONTEXT

Use with textbook page 347.

> **REMEMBER** Analyzing the historical context of a work of literature can make it more meaningful and easier to understand. To analyze historical context, pay attention to the events and the figurative language used to describe them in the work. Where and when did they take place? What was happening in the world at the time? Think about how the historical context relates to the story you are reading.

Read the passage. Then answer the questions.

> The streets of London were damp and muddy from the rain. The countess of Shropshire was helped out of her carriage by a footman. Servants carried her luggage into the Savoy Hotel while men unhitched the horses from the carriage and led the horses into the stable. Inside the hotel, a thirteen-year-old girl tended to the fire. She was a new scullery maid and when she saw the countess, her jaw dropped. The girl had never been to school and could not read. She had no idea that such fancy people as the countess even existed.

1. What is your best guess as to when and where the passage is set?

   _____

2. Underline clues in the passage that helped you to understand when and where the story is set.

3. Why do you think the thirteen-year-old girl had never been to school?

   _____

   _____

4. How does the period in which the story is set help to explain why a thirteen-year-old girl hadn't attended school?

   _____

   _____

5. How can the skill of analyzing historical context help you to understand what you read?

   _____

   _____

Copyright © by Pearson Education, Inc.

Unit 5 • Reading 2

171

Use with textbook page 352.

Circle the letter of the correct answer.

1. The speakers in the poem "In Flanders Fields" are _____.

    a. the dead soldiers   **b.** the poppies   **c.** the grass in the field

2. In the poem "In Flanders Fields," the speakers throw _____.

    a. a flower   **b.** a torch   **c.** a ball

3. In "Anthem for Doomed Youth," the soldiers are compared to _____.

    a. guns   **b.** singers   **c.** cattle

4. The "Three Wonderful Letters from Home" came from the soldier's _____.

    a. mother, wife, and baby   **b.** boss, friend, and mom   **c.** grandpa, father, and son

5. In "Letter Home," the soldier's attitude is _____.

    a. very scared   **b.** accepting   **c.** sad

RESPONSE TO LITERATURE *Use with textbook page 353.*

Imagine that you are the soldier described in one of these poems. You are far away, fighting a war. What do you think the greatest challenge of being at war would be? Write a paragraph in which you explain your ideas.

_____

_____

_____

_____

_____

_____

_____

_____

_____

_____

GRAMMAR

Contrast and Opposition *Use with textbook page 354.*

> **REMEMBER** The words *but, on the contrary,* and *much as* introduce contrast or opposition. *But* is a coordinating conjunction and connects two phrases or a clause and a phrase. Use a comma only between two clauses or when the phrase with *but* begins the sentence.
> **Example:** I like jogging, but only in the morning.
> *On the contrary* is a transition. It connects two independent clauses, separated by a semicolon.
> **Example:** My dad thinks I like playing softball; on the contrary, I prefer soccer.
> *Much as* initiates an adverbial clause, separated from the main clause by a comma.
> **Example:** Much as I like cake, eating too much makes me sick.

Complete each sentence. Choose between the words of opposition in parentheses.

Example: (but/much as/on the contrary) People had hoped that World War I was the

war to end all wars, _____ *but* _____ World War II started faster than anyone could imagine.

1. (But/Much as/On the contrary) _____ the soldiers went to the front willing to fight, actual warfare in the trenches made many of them fear death.

2. (but/much as/on the contrary) They all hoped to survive the war,

_____ many of them would die at the front.

Finish each sentence using the word or phrase in parentheses. Make sure you use correct punctuation.

Example: (on the contrary) Receiving a letter from the front did not mean the soldier

was still alive; _*on the contrary, many letters arrived home after the soldier's*_

*death at the front* .

3. (but) Frank Earley's letters home were usually full of cheer, _____

_____.

4. (on the contrary) Despite the thoughtful tone, Frank Earley was not depressed; _____

_____.

5. (Much as) _____,
Frank Earley died from a wound to the chest.

Write to Compare and Contrast *Use with textbook page 355.*

This is the Venn diagram that Jessica completed before writing her paragraph.

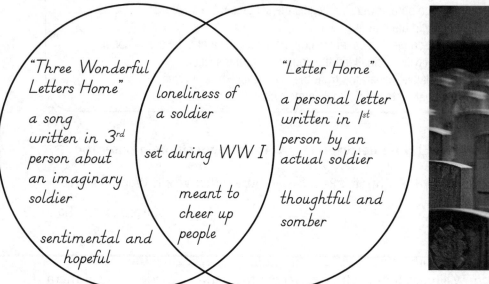

"Three Wonderful Letters Home"

a song written in 3rd person about an imaginary soldier

sentimental and hopeful

loneliness of a soldier

set during WW I

meant to cheer up people

"Letter Home"

a personal letter written in 1st person by an actual soldier

thoughtful and somber

Complete your own Venn diagram that compares and contrasts two things that are important to you, such as books, movies, sports, or foods.

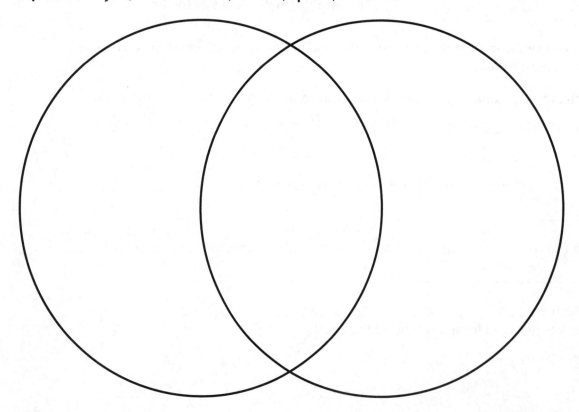

What can we learn from times of war?

READING 3: "In the Name of His Father"

VOCABULARY **Key Words** *Use with textbook page 357.*

Write each word in the box next to its definition.

consulate	diplomat	heroism	honor	lecture	refugees

Example: ___*refugees*___ : people who have been forced to leave their country, especially during a war

1. _____ : the official building where a foreign official lives and works

2. _____ : do something to show publicly that someone is respected and admired

3. _____ : very great courage

4. _____ : a long talk to a group of people about a particular subject

5. _____ : someone who officially represents his/her government in a foreign country

Use the words in the box at the top of the page to complete the sentences.

6. They heard a _____ about World War I.

7. Katie wants to be a _____ and represent the United States in a foreign country.

8. The soldier's _____ in battle showed her great bravery.

9. The _____ came across the border to escape the war.

10. We _____ heroes with awards and parades.

Read the paragraph below. Pay attention to the underlined academic words.

American movies about World War II often show the underline{exploits} of brave soldiers. There were certainly many brave American men who fought with underline{integrity} during the war. underline{Sympathetic} to the suffering in Europe and Asia, many gave their lives in the war. Indeed, World War II was a very tragic war. Though there is not an official underline{document} from the time that kept careful count of those who died, historians underline{estimate} that worldwide between fifty and seventy million people died because of the war.

Write the academic words from the paragraph above next to their correct definitions.

Example: ___*document*___ : a piece of paper that has official information written on it

1. _____ : the quality of being honest and having high moral principles

2. _____ : guess the value, size, number, etc., of something

3. _____ : showing that you understand how sad, hurt, lonely, etc. someone feels

4. _____ : brave and exciting actions

Use the academic words from the paragraph above to complete the sentences.

5. A birth certificate is an important official _____ .

6. The nurse was _____ to her patient's feelings.

7. We _____ that about 100 people will need shelter from the storm.

8. My uncle told the class about his amazing _____ during the war.

Complete the sentences with your own ideas.

Example: When my father has a special document, ___*he puts it in the safe*___ .

9. I estimate that the amount of time I spend doing homework is

_____ .

10. I respect people with integrity because _____ .

WORD STUDY The Suffix *-ness* *Use with textbook page 359.*

REMEMBER A suffix is a letter or group of letters added to the end of a word. A suffix often changes the word's meaning and part of speech. The suffix *-ness* describes a state, condition or quality. When you add *-ness* to an adjective, you form a noun. **Example:** *tender/tenderness.*
If a word has two or more syllables and ends in *y*, change the *y* into an *i* before adding the suffix *-ness.*
Example: *crazy/craziness*

Complete the chart by adding either the missing adjective or noun.

Adjective	+ ness = Noun
ready	*readiness*
1. dark	
2. useless	
3.	foolishness
4. sad	
5.	hopelessness
6.	friendliness
7.	bitterness

Add the suffix *-ness* to the adjectives in parentheses. Then write sentences with the new nouns.

Example: (short) *Stop exercising if you experience shortness of breath.*

 8. (gentle) _____

 9. (soft) _____

10. (bright) _____

11. (smooth) _____

12. (fit) _____

13. (kind) _____

14. (cleanly) _____

15. (careless) _____

REMEMBER When you draw conclusions, you better understand a text by putting clues together.

Read each selection and circle the most logical conclusion.

1. Leslie opened the windows wide. Then she put on the fan and made some lemonade. She drank the lemonade with a lot of ice.

   a. It is summer and very hot.   **b.** Leslie is an excellent cook.

2. Raul and Chin-Rae were fishing. Raul felt the tug of a huge fish on his line. The tug was very strong. The fish seemed to be very big. Chin-Rae stood up to pull the fish in. Then Raul saw Chin-Rae in the water.

   a. Chin-Rae has never fished before.   **b.** The fish pulled Chin-Rae into the water.

Read each paragraph and draw a conclusion.

3. Marco was painting his house yellow. At noon, Marco left the opened paint cans on the lawn. He went to eat lunch. He came out an hour later. He saw paint all over the lawn. The puppy was covered in yellow paint.

   What conclusion can you draw?

   _____

   _____

4. Dorrie put a soup bone on a dish. She put the dish on the counter. Her dog was sleeping next to the television. Dorrie took out the garbage. When she came back, the dog and the bone were gone.

   What conclusion can you draw?

   _____

   _____

5. How can the skill of drawing conclusions help you to better understand what you read?

   _____

   _____

COMPREHENSION *Use with textbook page 364.*

Circle the letter of the correct answer.

1. Chiune Sugihara is famous for _____.

   a. being a brave soldier   **b.** ruling Japan   **c.** helping save Jews from the Nazis

2. The Israelis have also honored _____.

   a. President Roosevelt   **b.** Oskar Schindler   **c.** Charles Lindbergh

3. Chiune Sugihara's actions were brave because _____.

   a. he put many people's needs before his own   **b.** he fought in the army   **c.** he saved his family

4. How did his own country treat Chiune Sugihara after World War II?

   a. honored him   **b.** put him in jail   **c.** took his job away

5. Chiune Sugihara comes from people who believe in _____.

   a. the power of money   **b.** the importance of honor   **c.** putting themselves first

EXTENSION *Use with textbook page 365.*

The chart lists five people linked to World War II. In the second column, list one fact about each person.

Person	Fact
Chiune Sugihara	
Oskar Schindler	
Raoul Wallenberg	
President Roosevelt	
Charles Lindbergh	

Passive Voice in the Present Perfect *Use with textbook page 366.*

> **REMEMBER** The passive voice focuses on the person or thing receiving the action in the sentence. The passive in the simple past is formed with *was/were* + past participle. A *by*-phrase identifies the performer of the action, but is not always needed.
> **Example:** We were driven to the movie theatre [by my parents].
> Use the present perfect when an action happened at an indefinite time in the past, or the action is still important now. Form it with *has/have been* + past participle.
> **Example:** The ball has been caught by the dog every time.

Read each pair of sentences. Put a ✓ next to the sentence in the passive voice.

Example: _____ Adolf Hitler ruled Germany during World War II.

_____✓_____ Germany was ruled by Adolf Hitler during World War II.

1. _____ Jews were forced to live in concentration camps.

_____ Hitler forced Jews to live in concentration camps.

2. _____ Sugihara knew that the German army was killing Jews.

_____ Sugihara knew that Jews were being killed by the German army.

Read each sentence. Rewrite each in the passive voice.

Example: The Allies defeated Hitler.

Hitler was defeated by the Allies.

3. The Allies had won the war.

_____

4. People all over the world honored the heroes of World War II.

_____

5. The government built a memorial in Washington for the veterans of World War II.

_____

Name _____ Date _____

Write a News Article *Use with textbook page 367.*

This is the 5Ws chart that Nicholas completed before writing his news article.

Who	Mrs. Bell's social studies class
Where	Washington D.C.
When	Last Thursday and Friday
What	Class trip
Why	Sightseeing

Complete your own 5Ws chart for a news article about a class trip, visit to a museum, or an issue.

Who	
Where	
When	
What	
Why	

What can we learn from times of war?

READING 4: From *Farewell to Manzanar*

VOCABULARY **Literary Words** *Use with textbook page 369.*

> **REMEMBER** **Diction** refers to a writer's choice of words. Diction can be formal or informal. **Tone** is the writer's attitude toward the subject. There are many tones: serious, funny, happy, sad, and so on.

Circle the words that best describe the diction and tone in each sentence.

Sentence	Diction		Tone	
"Four score and seven years ago our fathers brought forth on this continent a new nation, conceived in liberty. . . ."	(formal)	informal	(serious)	funny
1. Why did the man throw the clock out the window? He wanted to see time fly!	formal	informal	serious	funny
2. "Hey, you wanna grab lunch?" Jake asked. "Sure," Rick answered. "Gimme a minute."	formal	informal	positive	negative
3. Thunder rumbled! Lightning flashed! I heard a strange footstep. A scream rang out!	formal	informal	scary	comforting

Read the passage below. Answer the questions that follow.

> Quietly she put down the book. She looked slowly around the room. Then she tiptoed to the light switch and turned out the light. Standing in the darkened room, she thought about how this would be the very last night in her old bedroom.

4. Describe the diction of the passage above.

_____

5. Describe the tone of the passage above.

_____

VOCABULARY **Academic Words** *Use with textbook page 370.*

Read the paragraph below. Pay attention to the underlined academic words.

> A number of Japanese women and children moved to <u>isolated</u> towns in the mountains of Japan during World War II. At that time, Japanese cities were being bombed, so many people left the cities to <u>relocate</u> to a safer place. Many found a <u>temporary</u> place to live in small villages in the mountains. There was not much food, and <u>survival</u> was difficult, but a number of people were able to keep safe in isolated villages until the war ended.

Write the letter of the correct definition next to each word.

Example: __*b*__ isolated

_____ 1. relocate

_____ 2. survival

_____ 3. temporary

a. existing or happening only for a limited period of time

b. far away from other things

c. the state of continuing to live, especially after a difficult time or a dangerous situation

d. move to a new place

Use the academic words from the exercise above to complete the sentences.

4. The fair was _____ and soon moved to another town.

5. They wanted to _____ to a new place.

6. The operation will increase his chance of _____, so he can live longer.

7. The patient was _____ in the hospital so other people would not get sick.

Complete the sentences with your own ideas.

Example: Isolated people __*do not live near other people*__.

8. One thing I would need for survival in the woods is _____.

9. I want my family to relocate to the country of _____.

10. Something that is temporary in my life is _____.

> **REMEMBER** English has borrowed many words from other languages. Sometimes the words keep the same spelling, as in *chic* from the French. Other times, the words change spelling, as in *el lagarto*, the Spanish word for "lizard," which became *alligator* in English. Knowing the language a word comes from can help you spell, pronounce, and use the word correctly.

Look at the chart. Write your own definition for each borrowed word. Use a dictionary if needed.

Word	Borrowed from	Meaning
garage	French	*a place where cars are kept*
1. jaguar	Spanish/ Portuguese	
2. potato	Native American	
3. geyser	Icelandic	
4. orangutan	Malay	
5. saffron	Arabic	

Write a sentence that explains what each borrowed word below means. Use a dictionary if needed.

Example: beef (French) ___*Beef is the cooked meat from a cow.*___

6. canoe (Native American)

_____

7. typhoon (Chinese)

_____

8. macaroni (Italian)

_____

9. mammoth (Russian)

_____

10. cliché (French)

_____

READING STRATEGY | **ASK QUESTIONS** | *Use with textbook page 371.*

> **REMEMBER** When you ask questions as you read, you check your understanding of the text. Ask questions that start with these words: *Who, Where, When, What, Why.* Look for answers in the text.

Read each paragraph and answer the questions that follow.

1. Little Red Riding Hood went to visit her grandmother. On the way, she met the Big Bad Wolf. She told the Wolf where she was going. He followed her to Grandma's house.

   Who are the characters in the story?

   _____

   _____

2. A fisherman took his flute to the seashore. He played several songs. He hoped the fish would jump into his net. No fish came. At last, he put his flute down and threw his net into the sea. The fish jumped into his net! He said to the fish, "You would not come to me when I played music. Now that I have stopped, you jump into my net!"

   What happens in the story?

   _____

   _____

3. It was Saturday. Tom had a bucket of paint in one hand and a brush in the other. He looked at the fence sadly. The wood fence was so big! It would take all day to paint it.

   When is the story taking place?

   _____

4. Dorothy lived on the Kansas prairie. She lived with her Uncle Henry and her Aunt Em. Their house was small. The wood to build it had to be carried by wagon many miles.

   Where is the story taking place?

   _____

5. How can the skill of asking questions help you to better understand what you read?

   _____

   _____

Circle the letter of the correct answer.

1. The family's new home is a _____.

   a. shack **b.** beautiful house **c.** hotel room

2. The family's first task in their new home is to _____.

   a. take baths **b.** divide up the space for sleeping **c.** write letters to friends

3. The writer is glad that she is in a room with _____.

   a. a lot of heat **b.** her family **c.** strangers

4. Mama is sad because _____.

   a. she doesn't think her family should live in a shack **b.** she misses her family in Japan **c.** it rains all day

5. Woody is a good leader because _____.

   a. he is bigger than everyone else **b.** he will fight anyone who doesn't listen to him **c.** he keeps everyone's spirits up

RESPONSE TO LITERATURE *Use with textbook page 379.*

Draw a picture of the camp where the writer and her family lived. Use details from the story to help you show what it looked like.

GRAMMAR

Using Infinitives *Use with textbook page 380.*

> **REMEMBER** The infinitive is *to* plus the base form of a verb. The infinitive can be the subject, subject complement, or the object of a sentence. Infinitives can do many of the same things nouns do.
> **Examples:** You have *to talk* to your parents in times of trouble.
> Going to school *to study* was the best plan.
> You can use the infinitive to express a purpose. **Example:** I asked her *to study*.
> Certain adjectives and the words *too* or *enough* are often followed by the infinitive.
> **Examples:** We are too tired *to walk* to the store. It is good enough *to walk* every day for exercise.

Underline the infinitive in each sentence.

Example: My cousins are too polite <u>to complain</u>.

1. When I visited my cousins, they wanted me to feel at home.

2. They served too much food for them to eat.

3. To be the best requires great effort.

4. I've asked you to come several times.

5. Am I good enough to win this competition?

Combine each pair of sentences by using an infinitive.

Example: We are courageous enough. We can survive.

   We are courageous enough to survive.

6. They got some tools. They will fix things up.

   _____

7. She looked at her mother's face. She wanted to see her reaction.

   _____

8. I will make time. I need to finish this.

   _____

9. I want to visit France. I'd like to see the Eiffel Tower.

   _____

10. Let's hurry. We can catch the bus before it leaves.

   _____

Write a Problem-and-Solution Paragraph *Use with textbook page 381.*

This is the problem-and-solution chart that Dylan completed before writing his paragraph.

Problem
Internees had to share tiny rooms with others. There were knotholes in the wooden planks. At night it was too cold to sleep.

↓

Solution
Internees used blankets as room dividers. Internees covered the knotholes with tin can lids. They piled clothes on top of their beds at night.

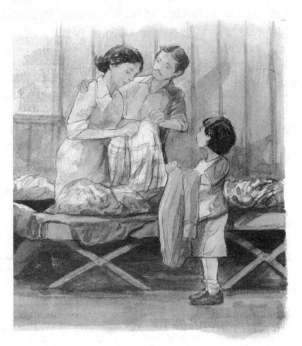

Complete your own problem-and-solution chart about a difficult situation that you or others solved.

Problem

↓

Solution

What can we learn from times of war?

UNIT 5

READING 5: "Sonnet to My Brother, a Soldier" and "He Died at His Post"

VOCABULARY **Etymology** *Use with textbook page 383.*

> **REMEMBER** **Etymology** explains where a word comes from, what it meant long ago, or how it once sounded. For example, *coffee* comes from the Arabic word *qawah*.

Use a dictionary to find the origin of each word listed in the chart. List its first recorded date of use and its original meaning.

Word and Definition	Origin	Date
Example: cow	*from the Latin word bos meaning "head of cattle"*	*before the 1100s*
sabotage:		
school:		
complain:		

Match the words in column A to the correct etymologies in column B. Use a dictionary if you need help.

Column A

Column B

1. bagel   Lithuanian *surus,* meaning "salty"

2. chalk   Middle High German *boug,* meaning "ring, bracelet"

3. scare   Greek *halixk,* meaning "small pebble"

4. sour   Old Norse *skjarr,* meaning "shy, timid"

5. friend   Old English *frēond,* meaning "to love"

> **REMEMBER** Poets choose the language they use very carefully. Their diction, or choice of words, is what makes a poem unique and imaginative. They also use **imagery,** or descriptions that appeal to the five senses (sight, sound, touch, taste, smell).

Read the poem below by William Butler Yeats, an Irish poet. He spent much of his childhood at Innisfree, where the poem's speaker plans to go. Use a dictionary to look up any words that are new to you. Then answer the questions below.

"The Lake Isle of Innisfree"

I will arise and go now, and go to Innisfree,
And a small cabin build there, of clay and wattles made;
Nine bean rows will I have there, a hive for the honey bee,
    And live alone in the bee-loud glade.

And I shall have some peace there, for peace comes dropping slow,
Dropping from the veils of the morning to where the cricket sings;
There midnight's all a glimmer, and noon a purple glow,
    And evening full of the linnet's wings.

I will arise and go now, for always night and day
I hear lake water lapping with low sounds by the shore;
While I stand on the roadway, or on the pavements gray,
    I hear it in the deep heart's core.

---

1. List two examples of imagery that appeal to the sense of sight.

_____

_____

2. List three examples of imagery that appeal to the sense of sound.

_____

_____

Name _____ Date _____

> **REMEMBER** **Figurative language** cannot be interpreted literally. It is imaginative. It is also often shaped by the time and culture in which it is written. A poet's choice to use a particular metaphor or symbol is frequently inspired by the time and culture in which he or she writes.

Read Oscar Wilde's poem "Impression du Matin" below. *Matin* **means "morning" in French. Use a dictionary to look up any words you don't know. Then answer the questions.**

> ### Impression du Matin
>
> The Thames nocturne of blue and gold
> Changed to a harmony in grey:
> A barge with ochre-coloured hay
> Dropt from the wharf: and chill and cold
>
> The yellow fog came creeping down
> The bridges, till the houses' walls
> Seemed changed to shadows, and St. Paul's
> Loomed like a bubble o'er the town.
>
> Then suddenly arose the clang
> Of waking life; the streets were stirred
> With country waggons; and a bird
> Flew to the glistening roofs and sang.
>
> But one pale woman all alone,
> The daylight kissing her wan hair,
> Loitered beneath the gas lamps' flare,
> With lips of flame and heart of stone.

1. What details suggest the time period of the poem?

_____

_____

2. What are some examples of figurative language? What details provide visual images?

_____

_____

> **REMEMBER** Figurative language is made up of different **figures of speech**. Some common figures of speech are **simile**, **metaphor**, **personification**, **symbol**, and **hyperbole**.

Read the following sentences. Identify the type of figurative language being used as a metaphor, simile, hyperbole, symbol or an example of personification.

1. Cameron stacked the dishes ten miles high. _____

2. The stars were smiling at me the day I made the soccer team. _____

3. His eyes were pools of darkness and mystery. _____

4. She's as sharp as a tack. _____

5. I was so tired—I could have slept for a hundred years. _____

6. Feeling the warm sunshine is like getting a hug from the world. _____

7. The tall, leafy tree watched over me. _____

8. Maya's expression was as sour as old milk. _____

9. She refused to dance—it was as though she were glued to her chair. _____

10. If I don't brush my hair twice a day, it turns into a bird's nest. _____

11. This locket reflects my love for my grandmother. _____

12. The man growled like a lion. _____

Using your knowledge of figurative language, create an original metaphor, a simile, and examples of personification and hyperbole. Look at the definitions on page 387 in your textbook if you need help.

1. metaphor – _____

2. simile – _____

3. personification – _____

4. hyperbole – _____

LITERARY ANALYSIS **Poetic Devices** *Use with textbook page 388.*

> **REMEMBER** Poetic devices like **meter**, **rhyme scheme**, and **stanza** help explain how a poet expresses his or her ideas.

Identify each poetic device defined below. Write *meter, rhyme scheme,* or *stanza* on the line following each.

1. A unit within a poem, similar to a paragraph, is called a _____.

2. The recurring rhythmical pattern of stressed and unstressed syllables is called

   _____.

3. The way a poem's rhymes are arranged is called _____.

Using your knowledge of rhyme scheme, write lines of poetry that reflect the patterns listed below.

1. aabb

   _____

   _____

   _____

   _____

2. abab

   _____

   _____

   _____

   _____

Write two lines of poetry. Make the syllables alternate between stressed and unstressed syllables.

   _____

   _____

Capitalization *Use with textbook pages 392–393.*

> **REMEMBER** Proper nouns name specific people, places, and things and should be capitalized. Some examples of proper nouns are people's names, the names of languages, cities, states, months, holidays, and published works. You should also use **capitalization** at the beginning of a sentence, at the beginning of a quotation, and when referring to yourself with the word *I.*

Using the lines below, rewrite this paragraph with correct capitalization.

next year i plan to start looking at different colleges to apply to. I've been looking at lots of books on picking a college, such as <u>college: how to pick the right one</u> and <u>higher education admissions.</u> I would love to go to school in boulder, colorado. it's a great city. My cousin sarah goes to school in denver. it would be fun to live in a new place but still have family nearby. I am a little bit afraid of being on my own in a new place. but my mom says that i should "get focused on long-term goals" and decide which schools have programs I'm really interested in. to be honest, I'm not sure what type of program or career would be right for me. i'm interested in learning new languages, especially french or chinese.

_____

_____

_____

_____

_____

_____

_____

_____

_____

_____

_____

WRITING **Write a Poem** *Use with textbook pages 394–395.*

Before you plan the content and structure of your poem, spend some time deciding the topic of your poem. You also need to think about the topic and also about the message you will send. Remember, a poem can be on any topic. Choose something that is important and meaningful to you.

Here are some general topics to help you brainstorm: friendship, family, relationships, community, growing older, work, memories, questions about life, challenges you've had.

Answer the following questions to get started choosing a topic.

What topic interests you?	
Why is it important to you?	
What message do you want to send to the reader?	
What examples, experiences, or feelings do you have about this topic?	
What details can you include to make the topic interesting to the reader?	

> **REMEMBER** A **poem** should combine all of the necessary poetic elements (language, structure, meaning) with your own personal vision. What your poem says and how it says it are up to you—the poet.

List your ideas for the content, structure, and language of your poem below. The different sections will help guide you.

Topic/Theme of Poem	Poetic Form and Rhyme Scheme
I will write about my hope that there will be fewer wars in the future and more peace.	**Form** *Sonnet* **Rhyme Scheme** *abab cdcd efef gg*
Examples/Details *There are too many wars going on that could potentially be resolved without violence.*	
Ways to Use Figurative Language (symbol, metaphor, simile, personification) *Image of open arms can symbolize desire for peace; clenched fist can symbolize war*	

Complete your own chart below.

Topic/Theme of Poem	Poetic Form and Rhyme Scheme
	Form **Rhyme Scheme**
Examples/Details	
Ways to Use Figurative Language (symbol, metaphor, simile, personification)	

EDIT AND PROOFREAD   *Use with textbook page 404.*

Read the paragraph below carefully. Look for mistakes in spelling, punctuation, and grammar. Correct the mistakes with the editing marks on Student Book page 553. Then rewrite the paragraph correctly on the lines below.

> Today, a famous writer came to visit our class. I was glad to meet the writer because I think I wants to be a writer when I grow up. The writer told us about the happyness she gets from her job. she writes stories poems and articles. We liked her stories about pets and we asked questions about these. I thought stories would be easy to write but on the contrary the writer said they are very difficult? I showed her some of my stories. She read the ones about my family and said they were very good. Her kindness made me feel good, and I thanked her courteouslly. Maybe I will be a famous writer some day

_____

_____

_____

_____

_____

_____

_____

_____

_____

Underline the vocabulary items you know and can use well. Review and practice any you haven't underlined. Underline them when you know them well.

Literary Words	Key Words		Academic Words	
figurative language	alliance	consulate	neutral	document
personification	armistice	diplomat	resources	estimate
diction	assassination	heroism	technology	exploits
tone	civilians	honor	tension	integrity
	surrendered	lecture	vehicles	sympathetic
	trenches	refugees	context	isolated
			create	relocate
			impact	survival
			similar	temporary

Put a check by the skills you can perform well. Review and practice any you haven't checked off. Check them off when you can perform them well.

Skills	I can . . .
Word Study	☐ recognize word roots. ☐ recognize and spell homophones. ☐ spell words with the suffix *-ness*. ☐ recognize and spell borrowed words. ☐ use etymology. ☐ use concept maps.
Reading Strategies	☐ identify cause and effect. ☐ analyze historical context. ☐ draw conclusions. ☐ ask questions.
Grammar	☐ use appositives. ☐ use words that show contrast and opposition. ☐ use passive voice in the present perfect. ☐ use infinitives. ☐ capitalize nouns.
Writing	☐ write a cause-and-effect paragraph. ☐ write a paragraph that compares and contrasts. ☐ write a news article. ☐ write a problem-and-solution paragraph. ☐ write a poem. ☐ write an expository essay.

Visual Literacy: Smithsonian American
Art Museum *Use with textbook pages 406–407.*

LEARNING TO LOOK

Look at *Save Freedom of Speech* by Norman Rockwell on page 406. Cover the right half of the painting with a blank sheet of paper. The standing man should be hidden. You should see the older man's face. Write down three observations about the older man. State facts, not opinions.

Older man

Example: *He is looking up.* _____

1. _____

2. _____

3. _____

Cover the left part of *Save Freedom of Speech* with a blank piece of paper. You should be able to see the standing man. Write down three observations about the standing man. State facts, not opinions.

Standing man

4. _____

5. _____

6. _____

INTERPRETATION

Look at *Save Freedom of Speech* by Norman Rockwell again. Write down how the details you observed for the "Learning to Look" exercise relates to the rest of the work of art.

Example: *The standing speaker has the attention of those sitting.* ____

_____

_____

_____

_____

Look at *Diary: December 12, 1941* by Roger Shimomura on page 407. Imagine that you have found the diary on the table in the painting. You open it and read it. Read the following Who, Where, When, What, Why, and How questions. Answer them based on what the author of the diary might have written.

1. **Who** is this woman?

   _____

   _____

2. **Where** is she going?

   _____

   _____

3. **When** will she return home?

   _____

   _____

4. **What** will she bring with her?

   _____

   _____

5. **Why** is she leaving?

   _____

   _____

6. **How** will she stay in contact with her friends?

   _____

   _____

What makes animals so amazing?

READING 1: "The Parrot Who Wouldn't Say 'Cataño'"

VOCABULARY   **Literary Words** *Use with textbook page 411.*

> **REMEMBER** An **archetype** is a type of character or a situation that appears often in literature.
> **Example:** a wise old teacher
> A **foil** is a character who is nearly opposite from another character.
> **Example:** A young, arrogant student could be a foil for a wise old teacher.

Look at each character described below. Write *A* if the character is an archetype and *NA* if it is not. (Ask yourself if it appears in literature.)

Archetype?	Character
A	a hardworking, loyal servant or employee
1.	a young couple in love who are kept apart by fate
2.	a character who likes to cook
3.	a beautiful princess in trouble
4.	a character who speaks seven languages
5.	a penniless orphan

Read the list of foils. Write the correct archetype from the box above next to the foil.

Archetype	Foil
a penniless orphan	a mean stepparent
6.	an old witch
7.	two sets of parents who don't want their children to get married
8.	a lazy, unappreciative master or boss

Choose two pairs from the box above and write a sentence about each.

9. _____

10. _____

Read the paragraph below. Pay attention to the underlined academic words.

Amy and Maria were childhood friends, but there was a huge contrast between their personalities. Maria was always careful and organized, but for Amy it was a challenge not to lose things. Maria let Amy borrow her sweater, even though she was very attached to it. When Amy lost the sweater, she was afraid of Maria's response. Maria didn't get angry. However, as a consequence of what happened she stopped letting Amy borrow her clothes.

Write the academic words from the paragraph above next to their correct definitions.

Example: _____*response*_____: something that is said, written, or done as a reply to something else

1. _____: something that happens as a result of a particular action

2. _____: strongly connected to someone or something

3. _____: something new, exciting, or difficult that needs a lot of skill and effort to do

Use the academic words from the paragraph above to complete the sentences.

4. The dogs barked in _____ to the noise of the car.

5. Hiking to the top of the mountain was quite a _____.

6. After taking care of my friend's pet bunny, I can't help but feel _____ to it.

7. As a _____ of not doing his homework, Michael got detention.

Complete the sentences with your own ideas.

Example: In response to the applause, _*I got up from the piano and bowed*_.

8. A consequence of not working hard is _____.

9. Something that is a challenge for me is _____.

10. When I was a child, I was attached to _____.

Name _____ Date _____

WORD STUDY **Suffixes** *Use with textbook page 413.*

> **REMEMBER** A suffix is a letter or group of letters added to the end of a word.
> The suffix *-en* means *to become*. It can turn an adjective into a verb. **Example:** black/blacken
> The suffix *-ful* means *having a quality*. It can turn a noun into an adjective. **Example:** sorrow/sorrowful
> The suffix *-ward* means *in the direction of*. It can turn a noun or preposition into an adverb.
> **Example:** west/westward
> The suffix *-ance* means *the act of*. It can turn a verb into a noun. **Example:** deliver/deliverance

Circle the suffix, and write *V* if the word is a verb, *N* if it is a noun, *A* if it is an adjective, and *ADV* if it is an adverb.

Examples: ___*A*___ cheer(ful)   4. _____ onward

1. _____ assistance   5. _____ useful

2. _____ sweeten   6. _____ westward

3. _____ helpful   7. _____ defiance

Create new nouns, verbs, adjectives, or adverbs by adding the correct ending. Then write a definition.

Example: Turn the verb *defy* into a noun.   *defiance: the act of defying*

 8. Turn the verb *perform* into a noun.   _____

 9. Turn the adjective *hard* into a verb.   _____

10. Turn the noun *fright* into an adjective.   _____

11. Turn the noun *hope* into an adjective.   _____

12. Turn the adjective *wide* into a verb.   _____

13. Turn the preposition *in* into an adverb.   _____

14. Turn the noun *beauty* into an adjective.   _____

15. Turn the adjective *light* into an adjective.   _____

> **REMEMBER** Connecting ideas in a text will help you to understand what an author is trying to convey.

Read the passage and answer the questions that follow.

> Julia was getting dressed for her Sweet Sixteen party. Her friend Maria had come over early to help.
>
> "Oh! I love your dress!" said Maria.
>
> "Thanks. My mom took me shopping last week to find it. I think we went to every store in the mall. I was beginning to think I wouldn't find anything!"
>
> "I had the same problem with my Sweet Sixteen dress. You have to find something special. You only have one 16th birthday! And," Maria added, "all our friends are coming."
>
> "Don't make me nervous," said Julia. "I could hardly sleep last night."
>
> "Oh, don't worry. It'll be great. I was nervous before my party. But then, when it starts, you don't even think about it. You'll be having so much fun!"
>
> "I hope so," said Julia. She looked at herself in the mirror. She loved her dress.
>
> "Are you ready?" asked Maria.
>
> "I think so. Let's go!" said Julia.

1. What roles do the characters play in each other's lives?

   _____

2. How are the birthday parties connected?

   _____

3. How are the character's attitudes about the party the same?

   _____

4. What is the main point of the passage?

   _____

5. How can the strategy of connecting ideas help you when reading a story or text?

   _____

COMPREHENSION   *Use with textbook page 418.*

Choose the best answer for each item. Circle the letter of the correct answer.

1. The parrot refused to say the name of _____.

   a. the sailor   **b.** the town   **c.** the poultry farmer

2. The sailor told the poultry farmer that if he could teach the parrot to say Cataño, the

   farmer could _____.

   a. take her with him   **b.** buy her   **c.** keep her

3. When the poultry farmer threw the parrot out the window, she landed _____.

   a. in the chicken coop   **b.** on a rafter   **c.** in the corridor

4. The poultry farmer returned the parrot because _____.

   a. she wouldn't say Cataño   **b.** she upset his   **c.** he was leaving San Juan
                                        chicken coop

5. The poultry farmer is an archetype of a _____.

   a. rich, impatient man   **b.** poor, gentle man   **c.** handsome, talkative man

RESPONSE TO LITERATURE   *Use with textbook page 419.*

Imagine an alternative ending to the story and write it on the lines below.

_____

_____

_____

_____

Reduction of Adjective Clauses to Adjective Phrases

Use with textbook page 420.

REMEMBER A clause contains both a subject and a verb. A phrase does not contain both a subject and a verb. Both adjective clauses and adjective phrases modify nouns. Omit the relative pronoun and the form of *be* to turn an adjective clause into an adjective phrase.
Examples: I transferred to the new school *that was* built outside of town. (adjective clause)
I transferred to the new school built outside of town. (adjective phrase)

Underline the adjective clause in each sentence below.

Example: Parrots can learn to repeat the words and phrases <u>that are said to them</u>.

1. Other birds that are able to mimic sounds are songbirds and hummingbirds.

2. For many years, one scientist studied a parrot who was named Alex.

3. Alex, who was taught the names of objects, seemed to be intelligent.

4. Alex was an African gray, which is a parrot famous for copying human speech.

5. Was Alex demonstrating imitation, which is repetition based on understanding?

Rewrite each sentence. Replace the adjective clause with an adjective phrase.

Example: There is a lot of information that is available on the Internet.
    There is a lot of information available on the Internet.

6. Irene Pepperberg, who is a parrot expert, had been working with Alex since 1977.

    _____

7. Pepperberg named the parrot Alex, which is short for *avian learning experiment.*

    _____

8. Alex was over 30, which is middle-aged for a parrot.

    _____

9. Alex could create new words that are based on words in his vocabulary.

    _____

10. Alex, who was a fussy eater, preferred raw almonds to roasted ones.

    _____

WRITING

Write an Introductory Paragraph *Use with textbook page 421.*

This is the inverted pyramid that Micah completed before writing his paragraph.

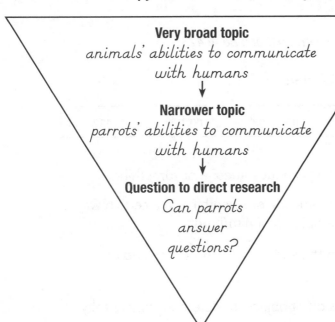

Very broad topic
animals' abilities to communicate with humans
↓
Narrower topic
parrots' abilities to communicate with humans
↓
Question to direct research
Can parrots answer questions?

Complete your own inverted pyramid to narrow your topic and write a question to direct your research.

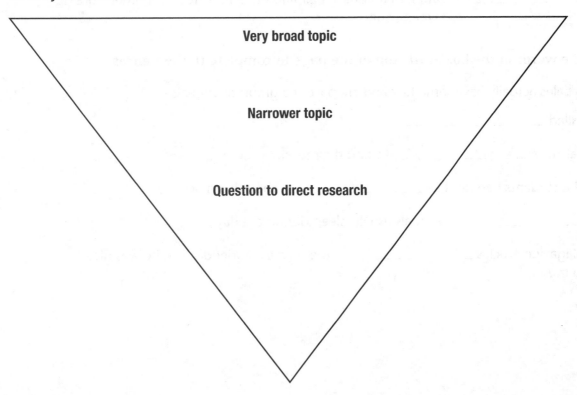

Very broad topic

Narrower topic

Question to direct research

What makes animals so amazing?

READING 2: "Getting to Know Real Bats"

VOCABULARY **Key Words** *Use with textbook page 423.*

Write each word in the box next to its definition.

| attitudes | echolocation | mammals | nocturnal | portray | wingspan |

Example: *attitudes* : opinions and feelings about someone or something

1. _____: describe or show someone or something in a certain way according to your opinion of him/her/it

2. _____: the distance from the end of one wing to the end of the other

3. _____: bouncing sounds off of objects to determine where they are located

4. _____: active during the night

5. _____: animals that have hair and drink milk from a mother's breast when young

Use the words in the box at the top of the page to complete the sentences.

6. Whales actually have some hair and are part of a group of animals

   called _____.

7. Bats use _____ to find their food.

8. The students had positive _____ about learning.

9. _____ animals usually sleep during the day.

10. Magazine articles _____ the man as unfriendly, but he was nice to me.

208 Unit 6 • Reading 2

Name _____ Date _____

VOCABULARY **Academic Words** *Use with textbook page 424.*

Read the paragraph below. Pay attention to the underlined academic words.

Many people are afraid of bats. This is often due to <u>ignorance</u>. Movies and TV shows often show bats as monsters that drink human blood, but this is not an <u>accurate</u> portrayal. In reality, bats do not attack innocent humans. Most bats are very <u>beneficial</u> to humans, because they eat mosquitoes and other insects. These are many different kinds of bats, and many have fascinating <u>features</u>.

Write the letter of the correct definition next to each word.

Example: __*d*__ features

_____ **1.** beneficial

_____ **2.** ignorance

_____ **3.** accurate

a. exactly correct

b. lack of knowledge or information about something

c. good or useful

d. parts of something that stand out because they seem important, interesting, or typical

Use the academic words from the exercise above to complete the sentences.

4. He showed his _____ of history when he said World War II happened in 1990.

5. Taking a vitamin can be _____ for your health.

6. My computer has some _____ that I don't even use.

Complete the sentences with your own ideas.

Example: My ignorance of __*the rules*_____ caused __*me to lose the game*_____.

7. The most interesting feature of my personality is _____.

8. I find it beneficial to _____ before a test.

9. I always check the _____ to make sure it is accurate.

10. One time my ignorance of something caused _____.

Unit 6 • Reading 2

Copyright © by Pearson Education, Inc.

Hyphenated Words *Use with textbook page 425.*

> **REMEMBER** Hyphens are one way to connect two or more words to create a single new meaning. Hyphenated words can describe, or modify, a noun. Use a hyphen if two or more words are used before a noun to express one idea.
> **Example:** The actor was well known. The *well-known* actor starred in new movie.
> It is often necessary to check a dictionary to find out if a hyphen should be used.

Transform the phrases using hyphenated words before the noun.

Example: the woman with red hair = *the red-haired woman*

1. a movie with a low budget = _____

2. a project that is after school = _____

3. a boy who is twelve years old= _____

4. a horse that is trained well = _____

5. a company with a high profile = _____

6. jeans covered with dirt = _____

7. eggs that are boiled until they are hard = _____

Write sentences using the hyphenated words in parentheses.

Example: (ebony-colored) *I bought an ebony-colored desk.*

8. (dark-eyed) _____

9. (well-paid) _____

10. (cold-blooded) _____

11. (highly-recommended) _____

12. (meat-eating) _____

13. (all-American) _____

14. (first-rate) _____

15. (left-handed) _____

READING STRATEGY | EVALUATE NEW INFORMATION

Use with textbook page 425.

> **REMEMBER** When you evaluate new information in a text, you can summarize what you've read, identify the author's purpose, take notes, and ask yourself questions to help you evaluate the information.

Read the paragraph and answer the questions that follow.

> The green movement is very popular in the United States. "Green" refers to products and living habits that are gentle to the environment and improve air quality. Green activities include building construction that limits waste and creates less pollution. Cars that run on electricity and gas are considered green because they make less pollution. Turning out lights, using less heat and cooling indoors, and recycling are green habits people can practice.

1. Summarize the passage in one sentence.

_____

_____

2. What is the author's purpose for writing?

_____

3. Give one example of a "green activity."

_____

_____

4. Did you find the paragraph informative? Why or Why not?

_____

5. How can the strategy of evaluating new information help you as a reader?

_____

_____

Choose the best answer for each item. Circle the letter of the correct answer.

1. The two main groups of bats are called _____.

   a. real bats and   b. megabats and microbats   c. bumblebee bats and
      imaginary bats   vampire bats

2. Small, insect-eating bats can tell where mosquitoes and other flying insects are by using _____.

   a. their eyes   b. their teeth   c. echolocation

3. Bats often snarl in photographs because they are _____.

   a. rabid   b. scared   c. hungry

4. Merlin Tuttle took pictures of bats eating _____.

   a. minnows   b. mosquitoes   c. mammals

5. The belief that bats commonly carry rabies is _____.

   a. a new idea   b. true   c. not true

EXTENSION *Use with textbook page 433.*

Choose five different types of bats and do research on each one. In the chart, write what each kind eats.

Bat species	What it eats
Egyptian fruit bat	fruit juices and flower nectar

GRAMMAR

Relative Pronouns as Subjects *Use with textbook page 434.*

> **REMEMBER** Adjective clauses describe nouns or noun phrases. Relative pronouns are the subjects of adjective clauses. *Who, that, which,* and *whose* are relative pronouns. *That* and *which* refer to things and other animals. *Whose* shows possession.

Underline the relative pronouns in each sentence. Then circle the noun or noun phrase modified by the adjective clause.

Example: Bats have (flexible wings,) which allow them to change direction easily

1. Scientists who study the way bats fly have learned a great deal.

2. Most mammals have heavy bones, which are not good for flight.

3. The ancestors of bats had fingers, which could be used to grasp things.

4. The air force would like to design an aircraft whose flight is like a bat's.

5. A machine that flies like a bat could be useful.

Combine each sentence by using the relative pronoun in parentheses.

Example: (which) An elephant is huge. It is the only mammal with a trunk.

An elephant, which is the only mammal with a trunk, is huge.

6. (that) Bats are mammals. They can fly.

_____

7. (whose) An aardvark is a mammal. Its home is in Africa.

_____

8. (who) Some people don't know the true nature of bats. They are afraid of them.

_____

9. (which) The blue whale is the largest animal on earth. It is bigger than any dinosaur.

_____

10. (who) People are mammalogists. They study mammals.

_____

Write Classifying Paragraphs *Use with textbook page 435.*

This is the T-chart that Leah completed before writing her paragraph.

Megabats	Microbats
larger	smaller
have long noses	small eyes
called flying foxes	don't see as well
large eyes can see day or night	active at night
use sight and smell to find food	use echolocation to find food
eat fruit	eat insects
live in Africa, Asia, Australia	many more species

Complete your own T-chart to classify a group of animals.

UNIT 6 — What makes animals so amazing?

READING 3: "The Bat" / "A Narrow Fellow in the Grass" / "Daybreak" / "Birdfoot's Grandpa"

VOCABULARY **Literary Words** *Use with textbook page 437.*

> **REMEMBER** **Similes** and **metaphors** are types of figurative language. **Similes** are comparisons that use the words *like* or *as*.
> **Example:** She can run like the wind.
> **Metaphors** are comparisons in which one thing is spoken about as though it were something else.
> **Example:** Life is a journey.

Label each sentence as an example of a simile or a metaphor.

Simile or Metaphor?	Sentence
simile	What you need to do is as clear as day.
1.	I'm as hungry as a bear.
2.	She has a heart of gold.
3.	My hands were as cold as ice.
4.	The test was a breeze.
5.	The idea was a slam dunk.

Write a sentence using a simile or a metaphor that describes each of the animals below. Label it as a simile or metaphor.

Animal	Sentence
Example: fish	*She swims like a fish. (simile)*
6. horse	
7. snake	
8. owl	
9. kitten	
10. fox	

Read the paragraph below. Pay attention to the underlined academic words.

Our teacher gave <u>explicit</u> guidelines for the research paper. The report had to be at least five pages long and be about a sea animal. It was <u>implicit</u> that it would require much time and research to earn a good grade. I chose to write my report on the octopus. The octopus is interesting because it can make itself appear <u>invisible</u> by blending into its surroundings. I gained an <u>appreciation</u> for this incredible animal after doing all my research.

Write the academic words from the paragraph above next to their correct definitions.

Example: _____*implicit*_____: suggested or understood but not stated directly

1. _____: an understanding of the importance, meaning, or beauty of something

2. _____: expressed in a way that is very clear and direct

3. _____: not able to be seen

Use the academic words from the paragraph above to complete the sentences.

4. The tiger's striped coat made it nearly _____ to its prey.

5. It is _____ that you'll stay home only if you are sick.

6. Your mother was _____ when she said to be home in time for dinner.

7. She has an _____ of classical violin music.

Complete the sentences with your own ideas.

Example: Thanks to your explicit directions, _____*we never got lost*_____.

8. If I could make myself invisible, I would _____.

9. I came early because I had explicit instructions to _____

_____.

10. I have an implicit agreement with my _____ to

_____.

WORD STUDY Words with Double Letters *Use with textbook page 439.*

> **REMEMBER** When adding *-ed, -er, -est,* and *-ing* to base words, the consonants *b, d, g, l, m, n, p, r,* and *t* must be doubled if the word ends on a consonant-vowel-consonant pattern.
> **Example:** *glad/gladder* but *bold/bolder.*

Write a ✓ next to the word that is spelled correctly.

Example: hit: ___✓___ hitting _____ hiting

1. wet: _____ weter _____ wetter

2. trim: _____ trimmest _____ trimest

3. sit: _____ sitting _____ siting

4. stare: _____ staring _____ starring

5. top: _____ toping _____ topping

6. kid: _____ kidding _____ kiding

7. fan: _____ faned _____ fanned

Look at the chart. Add *-ed, -er, -est,* or *-ing* to create a new word.

Base word	Suffix	New word
8. drag	*-ed*	*dragged*
9. dig	*-ing*	
10. grab	*-ed*	
11. bat	*-er*	
12. swim	*-ing*	
13. long	*-est*	
14. hop	*-ing*	
15. hot	*-er*	
16. end	*-ed*	

> **REMEMBER** When you read a poem aloud, you can hear the poem's rhythm and the sounds of its words.

Read the poem and answer the questions that follow.

I like to go to the city at night,
To watch the people, the cars, and light.
I hear horns, hoards, and haste,
Cars and people moving in a fast pace.

Back at home, when I'm resting in bed,
Pictures from the evening race 'round my head.
I smile happily thinking of the sound and sight,
From my walk through the city at night.

1. What are the rhyming words in the poem?

_____

_____

2. Is the rhythm of the poem slow or fast?

_____

3. Which words begin with the same letter or sound?

_____

4. What is the overall feeling of the poem when you read it aloud?

_____

_____

5. How can the strategy of reading aloud help you understand a poem?

_____

_____

COMPREHENSION   *Use with textbook page 444.*

Choose the best answer for each item. Circle the letter of the correct answer.

1. According to the poem "The Bat," when most of us see a bat we _____.

   a. think it's dead   **b.** feel afraid   **c.** think it's crazy

2. The poem "A Narrow Fellow in the Grass" is about _____.

   a. Emily Dickinson   **b.** a boy   **c.** a snake

3. According to "Daybreak," starfish sink into the mud by _____.

   a. sunset   **b.** daybreak   **c.** nightfall

4. In "Birdfoot's Grandpa," the old man saved _____.

   a. children   **b.** raindrops   **c.** toads

5. A theme throughout all the poems is _____.

   a. sadness about the earth   **b.** a connection the poet feels with nature   **c.** how animals are mistreated

RESPONSE TO LITERATURE   *Use with textbook page 445.*

Read the poems again and choose one. Write your own poem about the same kind of animal. Try to use similes and metaphors.

_____

_____

_____

_____

_____

Typical and Atypical Word Order *Use with textbook page 446.*

> **REMEMBER** In English, the typical, or usual, word order is subject / verb / object. Typically, adjectives appear before the nouns they modify. **Example:** Maria eats ice cream.
> Poets often write sentences with a different, or atypical, word order.
> **Example:** Maria happy, eats ice cream.

Read the word order in each sentence below and write *typical* or *atypical*.

_____ 1. The wide-awake snake slithered along the lake.

_____ 2. Alongside me hopped the toad into the road.

_____ 3. The grasshopper stopped atop a rock.

_____ 4. A grand achievement of engineering is the wingspan of a bat.

_____ 5. The dragonfly hovers over a pond like a helicopter.

Form a sentence from each group of words and phrases below. Follow the directions in parentheses.

Example: (Use atypical word order.) cat / the dangerous / green-eyed / creeps / through the grass

Through the grass creeps the dangerous green-eyed cat.

6. (Use atypical word order.) has / the toad / dry, warty skin

_____

7. (Use typical word order.) starfish / along the beach / collect / children / young

_____

8. (Use atypical word order.) the starfish / creature / is / an unusual

_____

9. (Use typical word order.) dogs / two big black / across the river / swam

_____

10. (Use typical word order.) through the night / frogs / the noisy / croak

_____

Name _____ Date _____

Support the Main Idea *Use with textbook page 447.*

This is the main-idea-and-details web that Dylan completed before writing his paragraph.

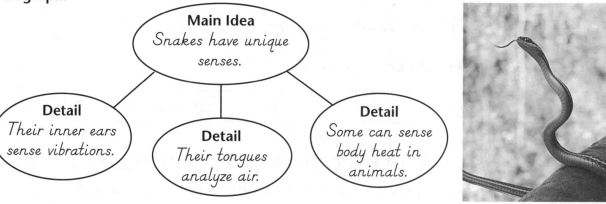

Main Idea
Snakes have unique senses.

Detail
Their inner ears sense vibrations.

Detail
Their tongues analyze air.

Detail
Some can sense body heat in animals.

Complete your own main-idea-and-details web for a paragraph about a pet, animals in the wild, or how animals are important in your life.

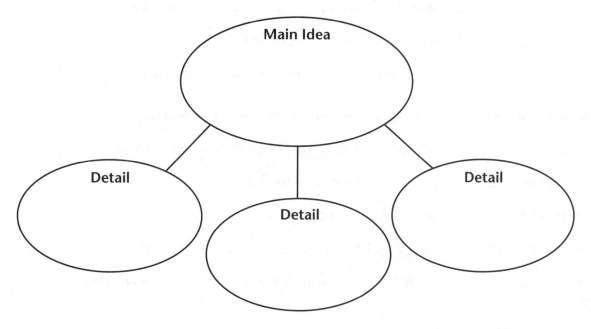

Main Idea

Detail

Detail

Detail

UNIT
6

What makes animals so amazing?

READING 4: From *The Chimpanzees I Love*

VOCABULARY   **Key Words** *Use with textbook page 449.*

Write each word in the box next to its definition.

| chimpanzees | commercial | existence | laboratories | sanctuaries | smuggle |

Example: ___*smuggle*___: to take something illegally from one place to another

1. _____: special rooms or buildings where scientists do tests and research

2. _____: African animals that are like a monkey without a tail

3. _____: relating to business and the buying and selling of things

4. _____: the type of life that someone or something has

5. _____: peaceful places that are safe and provide protection

Use the words in the box at the top of the page to complete the sentences.

6. _____, like humans, express emotions including joy and sadness.

7. Many wildlife _____ are open to tourists.

8. Scientists work in _____ to discover cures for diseases.

9. Cats that are kept as pets have a better _____ than stray cats.

10. People _____ endangered animals into the United States and then sell them.

Name _____ Date _____

VOCABULARY   **Academic Words** *Use with textbook page 450.*

Read the paragraph below. Pay attention to the underlined academic words.

> Jane Goodall has <u>committed</u> her life to studying and helping chimpanzees. She discovered that chimps are <u>intelligent</u> animals that use tools and can learn sign language. Goodall also discovered that many chimps are disappearing because of <u>inadequate</u> protection from human populations. Their forest habitats are being destroyed, and many chimps are hunted for food or sale. In 1977, Goodall formed the Jane Goodall Institute, which supports every approved <u>project</u> that helps chimps.

Write the letter of the correct definition next to each word.

Example: ___*b*___ project

_____ 1. inadequate

_____ 2. committed

_____ 3. intelligent

a. having a high level of ability to learn, understand, and think about things

b. a carefully planned piece of work

c. not good enough for a particular purpose

d. used all of the time and energy that you could in order to achieve something

Use the academic words from the exercise above to complete the sentences.

4. She was _____ to helping her team win the tournament.

5. He's the most _____ student in the school.

6. Our light clothing was _____ for the cold weather.

7. I will have to ask the librarian for some help with my school _____.

Complete the sentences with your own ideas.

Example: _____*Dolphins*_____ are intelligent animals.

8. I would like to do a class project about _____.

9. One thing I'm committed to is _____.

10. I think a school is inadequate if it does not _____.

Unit 6 • Reading 4

223

Frequently Misspelled Words

Use with textbook page 451.

> **REMEMBER** Common errors include: 1) mixing up letters, such as *wierd* for *weird;* 2) getting endings confused, such as *healthfull* for *healthful;* 3) mixing up spelling-sounds, such as writing *mimik* for *mimic;* 4) missing double letters, such as writing *mispeled* for *misspelled;* 5) adding double letters, as in *thankfull* for *thankful;* and 6) confusing words, such as *whether* for *weather.*

Spell each of the following words correctly. Check your work in a dictionary.

Example: Wenesday _____*Wednesday*_____

1. athalete _____

2. lightnning _____

3. usefull _____

4. beleive _____

5. sincerly _____

6. truely _____

7. nieghbor _____

8. accrross _____

9. panik _____

10. accidentaly _____

Read each sentence. Correct any misspelled words. Check your work in a dictionary.

11. I'm hopefull that our teem will win.

12. He tried to rememmber the gramar rule.

13. She didn't know much about iether buziness.

14. Mr. Myers axed us to read a similir book.

15. We weren't sure weather the whether would be good or bad.

READING STRATEGY | MAKE GENERALIZATIONS

Use with textbook page 451.

> **REMEMBER** When you make generalizations, you find things that are true for a number of points in a passage.

Read the paragraph and answer the questions that follow.

> All of the presidents of the United States have been men. Throughout history, women have campaigned to be both president and vice-president. However, a woman has never been elected into office. Many U.S. presidents have relied on help from their wives, as in the case of President Franklin Delano Roosevelt and First Lady Eleanor Roosevelt. Increasingly now, presidents employ powerful women to work closely with them, like Condoleezza Rice. These women provide expert advice and create important political strategies.

1. What generalization can you draw about the fact that all U.S. presidents have been male?

   _____

2. What generalization can you draw about the fact that women have run for president?

   _____

3. What generalization can you draw about the fact that there are women who have helped or worked for presidents?

   _____

4. Which generalization cannot be made from the passage above?
   a. Some women would like to be president.
   b. Important women have helped presidents.
   c. The presidents in the future will be men too.
   d. There are talented women who could be president.

5. How can the strategy of making generalizations help you as a reader?

   _____

Choose the best answer for each item. Circle the letter of the correct answer.

1. Chimpanzees can do many things that _____.

   a. termites can do   **b.** humans can do   **c.** dogs can do

2. One thing that chimpanzees cannot learn is how to _____.

   a. ride a bicycle   **b.** use sign language   **c.** speak words

3. Scientists use chimps to find out about human diseases because _____.

   a. their bodies are like ours   **b.** they can bite   **c.** they are adorable

4. Good zoos provide their chimpanzees with _____.

   a. car tires   **b.** small cages   **c.** different activities

5. Humans have often treated chimps _____.

   a. with cruelty   **b.** with respect   **c.** just like they were people

EXTENSION *Use with textbook page 459.*

Have you ever been to a zoo or seen pictures of animals in a zoo? Choose an animal in the zoo and write a paragraph about how you think that animal is treated. Could it be treated better?

_____

_____

_____

_____

_____

GRAMMAR

Gerunds and Infinitives *Use with textbook page 460.*

> **REMEMBER** Gerunds (the base form of a verb + *-ing*) and infinitives (*to* + the base form of a verb) are verb forms that can function as nouns. Gerunds and gerund phrases can be subjects, subject complements, objects of a verb, or objects of a preposition.
> **Examples:** *Walking* is beneficial to your health. A good form of exercise is *walking*.
> Infinitives and infinitive phrases can be subjects of a sentence or objects of a verb.
> **Examples:** *To study* for tests I have to have silence. For a test, I have *to study* in silence.

Read each sentence. Underline the gerund, gerund phrase, infinitive, or infinitive phrase.

Example: Chimpanzees can learn <u>to ride a bicycle</u>.

1. Another skill chimpanzees can learn is sewing.

2. Teaching people about chimpanzees is one of Jane Goodall's projects.

3. Chimpanzees use American Sign Language to communicate.

4. They learn by watching others.

5. Goodall is unhappy to see the mistreatment of chimpanzees.

Complete each sentence by adding the appropriate gerund or infinitive from the word box. Capitalize if needed.

to joke	to marry	asking	to fail	jogging

6. _____ is to make a serious commitment.

7. _____ is good exercise!

8. I learn best by _____ questions.

9. It is all right _____ if you succeed in the end.

10. This is no time _____.

WRITING

Include Quotations and Citations *Use with textbook page 461.*

This is the main-idea-and-details web that Adrian completed before writing his paragraph.

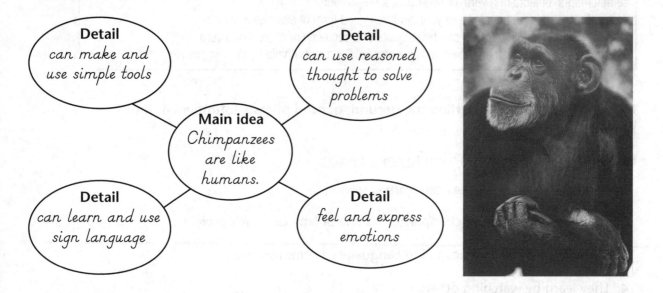

Complete your own main-idea-and-details web for a paragraph that includes quotations and citations.

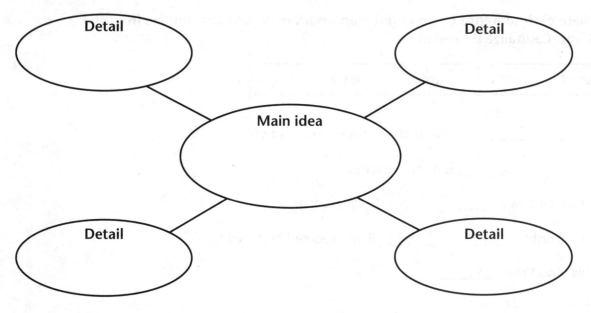

What makes animals so amazing?

UNIT 6

READING 5: "Caesar Kleberg: A Man Ahead of His Time"

VOCABULARY **Foreign Words and Phrases** *Use with textbook page 463.*

> **REMEMBER** Words from other languages often become part of everyday English. This happens when English lacks a word with exactly the same meaning. Use context clues to understand the meaning of these foreign words and phrases.

Column A contains some common foreign phrases. Use a dictionary. Write the letter of the correct definition in Column B on the lines in Column A.

Column A	Column B
1. _____ quid pro quo	**a.** conversation between two people
2. _____ bon appetit	**b.** something exchanged for something else
3. _____ tête-à-tête	**c.** enjoy your meal

Read the sentences. Use context clues to choose the foreign word or phrase from Column A above to fill in each blank.

1. The server said "_____" as she delivered our pasta dishes to the table.

2. My brother and I have a nice _____ arrangement—he gives me a ride to soccer practice, and I make his lunch.

3. After their argument, Maria and Sal made up and had a _____ over lunch.

> **REMEMBER** A **biography** tells the story of a person's life. Biographies are often short and filled with facts. A **literary biography** also gives facts about a person's life but is written in a literary style, like a story. Authors of literary biographies weave together factual information with descriptions of people's experiences.

Read the following items. Decide if each item is from a literary biography or a regular biography. On the lines provided, write a sentence or two to support your answers.

1. The Perkins School for the Blind, from which Helen Keller graduated, was founded in 1829 in Massachusetts.

   _____

   _____

2. Annie raised Helen's hand to her eyes in a questioning way, and Helen nodded energetically. The beads were sewed in the right place and Helen could not contain herself for joy.

   _____

   _____

3. The phrase "the miracle worker," which refers to Helen's teacher, Anne Sullivan Macy, was originally coined by writer Mark Twain.

   _____

   _____

4. Helen tumbled off the seat and searched under it until she found her aunt's cape, which was trimmed with large beads.

   _____

   _____

GRAMMAR

Using Negatives Correctly *Use with textbook page 469.*

REMEMBER Verbs can be used in the **negative form**. The negative form of a verb is made by adding *not*. To form the simple past in the negative, use *did not* + the base verb.

Write the negative form of these sentences on the lines below.

1. It snowed yesterday.

   _____

2. Otis loves hockey.

   _____

3. We will leave at 6 P.M.

   _____

4. Randall set the table.

   _____

5. You saw the newspaper.

   _____

6. Inez turned on the television.

   _____

7. We recited a funny poem.

   _____

8. You bought the pet food.

   _____

9. I spoke to Mr. Oliva.

   _____

10. You remembered your coat.

   _____

Using Contractions Correctly *Use with textbook page 469.*

> **REMEMBER** Contractions are the shortened forms of negatives and are used in informal speech and writing. The negative forms of helping verbs and modal verbs are also often contracted.

Rewrite the sentences using contractions.

1. They do not like taking tests.

   _____

2. You cannot tell the twins apart.

   _____

3. We will not leave till 1 P.M.

   _____

4. They do not work on Sundays.

   _____

5. He does not play the drums.

   _____

6. Tricia did not wash the dishes.

   _____

7. Cory will not type his report.

   _____

8. The flight was not on time.

   _____

9. They did not take their car.

   _____

10. You should not drive fast.

    _____

WRITING

Write an Interpretative Response *Use with textbook pages 470–471.*

Prepare to write your interpretative response by answering the questions below. Use your answers to make your outline.

Which details about Caesar Kleberg's life stand out as unusual or memorable?

_____

_____

How do these details relate to the biographer's main points about Caesar Kleberg?

_____

_____

Which sentences or details from the biography state facts? Which sentences or details state or suggest opinions?

_____

_____

Which sentences or details hint at the author's tone or attitude about the subject?

_____

_____

Where does the author use imagery, or word pictures?

_____

_____

How does the author draw you into the story of Caesar Kleberg's life, making it vivid and interesting?

_____

_____

Edit and Proofread *Use with textbook page 473.*

Read the excerpt from a student essay shown below. Then, on the lines provided, rewrite the passage. Edit and proofread the passage so that it reads more smoothly and follows the rules of grammar, spelling, usage, and mechanics.

> The biographer stress that Caesar Kleberg plays an important role in the development of the king ranch. For example, Caesar tracked down the source of a disease that kill many cattle started a program to eradicate ticks. Caesar and Bob Kleberg, Jr., also made a key contribution when they found out that there cattle needed a phosphorus suplement in there diet. A third important decision was draw up a set of game hunting rules. Caesar has noticed a decline in wildlife populations on the ranch. He wanted to make sure so wildlife like deer and turkeys were not over-hunted. According to Caesars rules, many animals and birds could be only hunted at certain times of year.

_____

_____

_____

_____

_____

_____

_____

_____

PREPARE AN ORAL REPORT

Finding Sources *Use with textbook page 474.*

Review the chart that Javier used when choosing a topic.

What I Already Know	What I Need to Know	Where I Might Find This Information
• *Many different types of animals live in the Arizona desert.*	• *How do the animals survive in the heat?*	• *an Arizona-based website that focuses on animals*
• *Animals survive because of adaptations.*	• *Do both mammals and reptiles live in the desert?*	• *a reference book of desert animal adaptations*

Complete your own chart before you begin your research report. Discuss your ideas with a partner.

What I Already Know	What I Need to Know	Where I Might Find This Information

PREPARE AN ORAL REPORT

Evaluating Sources *Use with textbook pages 475–477.*

Review the chart that Javier created while gathering information. He quoted the information, paraphrased it, and listed the sources in MLA format.

Information	Paraphrase	Source
"Arizona desert tortoises can live up to sixty years of age."	"Arizona desert tortoises can live almost as long as many humans (as long as 60 years)."	Collins, Marcus. "Arizona Desert Tortoises." <u>All About the Arizona Desert Tortoise</u> 10 Nov. 2009. Arizona Desert Project. 15 Nov. 2010 <www.arizonatortoiseproject.org>.

Complete your own chart as you prepare your research report.

Information	Paraphrase	Source

EDIT AND PROOFREAD *Use with textbook page 486.*

Read the paragraph below carefully. Look for mistakes in spelling, punctuation, and grammar. Correct the mistakes with the editing marks on Student Book page 553. Then rewrite the paragraph correctly on the lines below.

> The four frends planned their camping trip for Months. when the big day finally arrived, they put there backpacks into canoes and shoved off. They paddled across a Beautiful lake to an iland, took off thier backpacks and started to explore. They found rocks, trees, and chipmunks. Then the sun begun to set. It was time to set up the tents Each freind waited for one of the others to take a tent out of his backpack. But no one did. Despite all their planning, they had forgotten the tents! "It's okay. We'll sleep under the stars, they said. Unfortunately, it started to rain in the middle of the nite. Everybody got wet. but after they returned home they had fun sharing the story with their families and friends. It made the camping trip something they would always remember.

_____

_____

_____

_____

_____

_____

_____

_____

Underline the vocabulary items you know and can use well. Review and practice any you haven't underlined. Underline them when you know them well.

Literary Words	Key Words		Academic Words	
archetype	attitudes	chimpanzees	attached	appreciation
foil	echolocation	commercial	challenge	explicit
simile	mammals	existence	consequence	implicit
metaphor	nocturnal	laboratories	response	invisible
	portray	sanctuaries	accurate	committed
	wingspan	smuggle	beneficial	inadequate
			features	intelligent
			ignorance	project

Put a check by the skills you can perform well. Review and practice any you haven't checked off. Check them off when you can perform them well.

Skills	I can . . .
Word Study	☐ recognize and use suffixes. ☐ recognize and spell hyphenated words. ☐ recognize and spell words with double letters. ☐ recognize frequently misspelled words. ☐ recognize and use foreign words and phrases.
Reading Strategies	☐ connect ideas. ☐ evaluate new information. ☐ read aloud. ☐ make generalizations.
Grammar	☐ reduce adjective clauses to adjective phrases. ☐ use relative pronouns as subjects. ☐ use typical and atypical word order. ☐ use gerunds and infinitives. ☐ use negatives and contractions.
Writing	☐ write an introductory paragraph. ☐ write classifying paragraphs. ☐ support the main idea. ☐ include quotations and citations. ☐ write an interpretative response. ☐ write a research report.

Visual Literacy: Smithsonian American
Art Museum *Use with textbook pages 488–489.*

LEARNING TO LOOK

Look at *Ajax* **by John Steuart Curry on page 488. Write down six things you notice about the bull in this painting. State facts, not opinions.**

Example: *The bull is brown and white.* _____

1. _____

2. _____

3. _____

4. _____

5. _____

6. _____

INTERPRETATION

Look at *Game Fish* **by Larry Fuente on page 489. Link to http://americanart.si.edu/ collections/search/artwork/?id=32281 on the Internet. Look at the details of** *Game Fish.*

First Impressions
What words come to mind when you see this artwork?

Example: *playful* _____

_____

_____

Imagination
Imagine that you caught *Game Fish* **while fishing. What would you do with it?**

_____

_____

COMPARE & CONTRAST

Look at *Game Fish* by Larry Fuente and *Ajax* by John Steuart Curry again. Use these two artworks to complete the diagram below. Describe each piece of art in the outside sections of the diagram. Then list the similarities between the two artworks in the center where the two circles overlap.

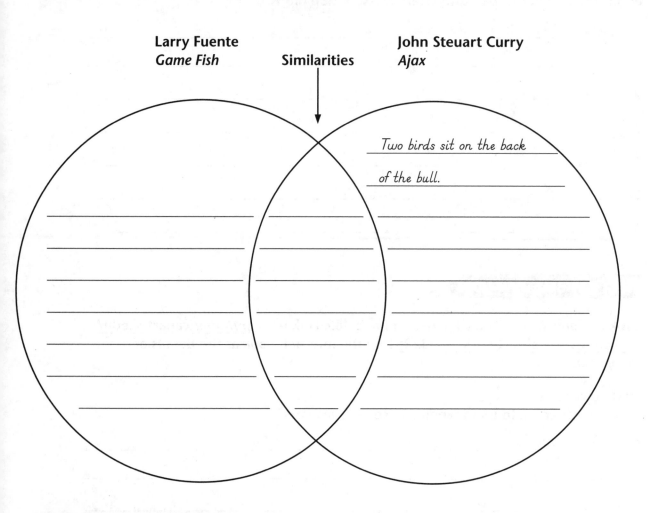

Larry Fuente
Game Fish

Similarities

John Steuart Curry
Ajax

Two birds sit on the back of the bull.

MEDIA LITERACY

Now that you have read about people's relationship with nature, go to www.LongmanKeystone.com for links to the Smithsonian website. Follow the online instructions to compare the artwork in your student book with other media that convey similar messages. Which messages are conveyed more directly through visual media? Which ideas are conveyed more effectively through print or audio?

TEST PREPARATION

Name _____ Date _____

DIRECTIONS
Read the selection. Then answer the questions that follow it.

Where the Sun Never Sets

Although it is the same sun that shines upon the same Earth throughout the globe and throughout the year, a single person situated at a different point of the globe experiences light and dark, day and night, in extraordinarily different ways. There are places where the daytime and nighttime hours are always the same. There are places where the sun doesn't shine at all for days and places where the sun doesn't set at all for days. This is because of the shape and tilt of the Earth as well as the way in which the Earth orbits the sun on its 365.25 day course.

At the equator, day and night are each exactly twelve hours long. This never changes, regardless of the season. The equatorial region does not experience a change at the summer (June 21) and winter (December 21) solstices like North America does. In the United States, the days are shortened until the winter solstice (the shortest day of the year) and lengthen from then until the summer solstice (the longest day of the year).

In the Arctic Circle, however, something else occurs during the solstices. In Barrow, Alaska, for example, the sun doesn't set for days around the summer solstice. During the winter solstice in Barrow, the sun never rises. Your location on Earth and the time of year can mean an endless summer day or an endless winter night.

---

1   Based on the information in the passage, what causes Barrow, Alaska, to experience long
    periods of daylight without darkness?
    A Its extreme temperatures
    B Its geographic location
    C Its weather patterns
    D Its relative distance from the sun

2   According to the passage, what is unusual about days and nights at the equator?
    F The hours of sunlight and darkness are always equal.
    G It is the part of Earth farthest away from the sun.
    H Its longer days contribute to its hot climate.
    J The summer and winter solstices do not occur there.

UNIT 1 TEST 2

DIRECTIONS
Read the selection. Then answer the questions that follow it.

A Difference in Viewpoint

C.J. and Micha had spent their entire day indoors working on a *collaborative* school project with another classmate, Troy. The three had come to an impasse because they could not agree on how the paper should be written. The topic was Benjamin Franklin, and all three had a different way of exploring this statesman who had done so many things in his life. Micha wanted to talk about his inventions and discoveries. C.J. wanted to focus on his work as an ambassador. Troy thought it best to write about his writings and quotations, all still popular today.

After a difficult discussion that had become somewhat *heated*, Troy suggested they step outside. The rain had finally stopped, and a distraction might help them all. As the three stepped out on the porch, they were stunned to see a perfect rainbow in the sky.

"It makes me think of how beautiful the world is, so full of life and mystery," said Troy. "I could write a poem about it."

"It makes me think about the laws of the universe and how simple rain can bend light into colors," said Micha.

"It makes me think about how people everywhere can all feel the same wonder and learn that their differences aren't really that different at all," said C.J.

"That's it!" yelled Micha suddenly. "I have the answer to our paper. What if we introduce Ben Franklin and then each write different parts of the paper, focusing on different aspects of his life and work," she said. "Then, we can write a page together about how each of his strengths made him a singularly great man."

The three loved the idea. They ran into the house and began writing outlines. It amazed them how a single event, like a rainbow or a person's life, could have so many different aspects that made it a single, amazing thing.

---

1 What does the word *collaborative* in the first paragraph most likely mean?
   A Not very important
   B Difficult to complete
   C Done by a group
   D Worth extra credit

2 What does the word *heated* in the second paragraph most likely mean?
   F Warm
   G Friendly
   H Academic
   J Angry

Name _____ Date _____

DIRECTIONS
Read the selection. Then answer the questions that follow it.

Smithville Needs a Community Garden

At the end of West Main Street there is a vast overgrown and trash-strewn lot where a mall once stood. This vacant lot has become a nuisance to our city. It invites car races, vandalism, and loitering. It is a refuge for all kinds of vermin that live in the tall weeds and trash piles. The city board is currently weighing options for the rehabilitation of that lot. Some want an apartment complex or a new shopping center with businesses. However, I suggest we turn that acre of dirt to good use for the city and grow a community garden.

A community garden is an area of public land on which a group of volunteers cultivate crops. There are no fewer than six gardening clubs in Smithville, all of whom would be excited for the opportunity to help with such a project. A community garden can provide healthy vegetables and fruits for low-income families. It reduces crime because the land is no longer vacant. It preserves open space, builds community, reduces the pollution caused by car exhaust, and a million other wonderful things. There are even grants available to fund a new community garden. The loss of tax revenue from building a private business on the lot is nothing compared to the problems another failed retailer on that land would bring.

I encourage the citizens of Smithville to come to the next board meeting and press the council to consider this excellent alternative use of that empty eyesore.

---

1 This passage is an example of what type of genre?
  A A science article
  B A newspaper editorial
  C An autobiography
  D An instruction manual

2 What possible objection to the community garden plan does the author NOT address in the passage?
  F The cost of starting and maintaining a community garden
  G Whether there will be enough volunteers for the garden
  H The loss of tax revenue from possible businesses on the lot
  J How the city will provide security against garden vandalism

UNIT 2 TEST 2

DIRECTIONS
Read the selection. Then answer the questions that follow it.

When You Were Young

When you were young, you sat in a field for hours looking at the shoots of grass. Now that you're grown, you mow instead of marvel.

When you were young, five minutes took hours and you made characters out of your hands to pass the time. Now that you're grown, a day lasts five minutes, and you call to make appointments while you wait for appointments.

When you were young, you laughed and you snickered at things that shouldn't be said in the classroom. Now that you're grown, you'd never dare giggle at meetings or lunches or dinners.

When you were young, you wanted to be grown. Now that you're grown, you want to be young.

Now that you're grown, cancel appointments and sit in a field while you stare at the plants.

Now that you're grown, keep the pockets of your suit lined with silly trinkets and toys.

Now that you're grown, remember you're young. You'll always be young until you stop growing.

1 What is the purpose of comparing youth and maturity in the passage?
   A To demonstrate the loss of play that can happen in adulthood
   B To persuade the reader that maturity is more important
   C To highlight the growth process in the human person
   D To underscore the need to take responsibility in life

2 What purpose do the last three lines of the poem serve?
   F To answer a question
   G To show regret
   H To give advice
   J To continue an argument

Test Preparation

UNIT 3 TEST 1

DIRECTIONS
Read the selection. Then answer the questions that follow it.

Do We Still Tell Fables?

All cultures have fictional tales that highlight both the requirements of their society and the consequences of breaking the rules. Aesop's fables are among the best known examples of the genre. Fables teach the listener how a culture operates and how to live in the best way possible with other people. Do we still tell fables in modern times? Some might say we do, but they go by a different name: urban legends.

An urban legend is a story about something that didn't really happen (though it may have some basis in fact), teaches a lesson about danger or justice, and is told as an absolutely true story. Often, the legend is given credibility, not by being repeated by an elder (like a fable), but because we hear them from friends who claim to know someone who knows the legend is true. Urban legends have common themes, but two seem predominant: fear of the unknown in the modern world and justice is always done, often in an ironic way.

Sometimes a legend is humorous, as in the man who thought his computer disk drive was a coffee cup holder. Sometimes they are more sinister, like the foreigner who warns of an impending disaster because of some kindness a person has done to him or her. Like a fable, every legend teaches a common lesson: society as we know it is weird and frightening. Be on your guard!

---

1 According to the passage, how are urban legends like fables?
   A They are both told as though they were true events.
   B They both teach their lessons with humor.
   C Both criticize the society in which they originate.
   D Both teach a lesson about the culture that created them.

2 Based on the information in the passage, what prompts people to tell and believe urban legends?
   F A desire to participate in the community
   G An ignorance of one's own culture
   H A fear of the unknown in the world
   J A desire to pass on a moral

Name _____ Date _____

DIRECTIONS
Read the selection. Then answer the questions that follow it.

A Misunderstood Serpent

(1) The diamondback water snake makes its home throughout much of Oklahoma and other Southwest regions. (2) It eats primarily frogs and fish and is often found lazily basking in the sun near a body of water. (3) It is a nonvenomous snake, meaning it is harmless to humans. (4) Venomous snakes release their toxins through tubes in their fangs. (5) While the diamondback water snake may attempt to bite if threatened, it does not produce venom. (6) It will produce a musk smell and snap at whatever threatens it.

(7) The problem the diamondback water snake has is that it looks a great deal like the extremely venomous cottonmouth snake. (8) Both snakes swim in the water, though the diamondback snake swims with only its head above the surface of the water. (9) The cottonmouth sidles through the water with its entire body on the surface. (10) This is the fastest way to tell the two reptiles apart. (11) However, because a cottonmouth is so poisonous to humans, it is best to get out of the water as fast as possible when you spot a snake in the water, no matter how it swims!

---

1 What does the word *basking* mean in sentence 2?
   A Enjoying a warm or pleasant place
   B Attacking an object nearby
   C Feeding on nearby grass
   D Laying eggs on a flat object

2 Based on the information in the passage, what is *venom*?
   F Simple saliva
   G A poisonous liquid
   H A foul smell
   J Rough scales

UNIT 4 TEST 1

DIRECTIONS
Read the selection. Then answer the questions that follow it.

The Pounding Heart

Hector tapped his badly chewed pencil against the edge of his desk. He tried to look as far to the right as he could without appearing to avoid looking to his left. Livia was sitting to his left, and Hector desperately wanted to ask her a question that he was also desperately afraid to ask. He tapped his pencil harder and faster until it fractured along a bite-line and fell to the floor. He bent to his left to grab it quickly and his head met with a hard object doing the exact same thing.

"Oooh! Ow!" Livia said, rubbing the side of her head. She started to laugh as she squinted through the pain. "Sorry. I thought I dropped something."

Hector, rubbing his head, laughed as well. Hector stared at her, in his mind saying the words he had rehearsed over and over to himself. If only he could say them out loud, he might be in heaven on Friday night. It would be a darkened gymnasium, but he would be in heaven, nonetheless.

"Hector?" Livia whispered.

Hector jumped. He'd been staring at her. "What?" he said.

"What, what? What do you want? You keep saying my name."

Hector had been completely unaware that he had been saying Livia's name out loud. He cleared his throat and a strange calm overcame him. He looked at her and smiled. She smiled back and his whole body relaxed. He leaned in and whispered his question.

"Yes," Livia said as she blushed. "I'd love to."

---

1 What question did Hector likely want to ask Livia?
   A If she would help him study for Friday's test
   B If she would watch him play basketball this week
   C If she would come to his house for a party
   D If she would go with him to a school dance

2 What is the setting of the story?
   F A gymnasium at night
   G A classroom during the day
   H The bleachers of stadium
   J A school cafeteria

UNIT 4 TEST 2

DIRECTIONS
Read the selection. Then answer the questions that follow it.

Caring for Your Heart with Your Head

Much has been written about proper heart health in recent years. Most people are aware of the importance of regular exercise, high fiber diets, healthy versus unhealthy fats, and the importance of maintaining a healthy body mass index (BMI). However, many people ignore the fact that stress exerts an incredible influence on your heart health. Often, when a doctor recommends that a patient reduce their stress level, the patient is at a loss. Life is stressful. How can I stop things from happening that are beyond my control?

What doctors need to say instead of "reduce your stress" is "counteract your stress." There are many things you can do to ease the stress in your life and all of them boil down to one word: joy. Doing something you love, even if it is for a brief period every day, eases your sensation of stress and calms you. Talking with friends, reading a book, taking a walk, working at a hobby, playing with a pet: these are activities that are not only joyful, but that also keep your heart healthy. When you are feeling your most stressed, the best thing you can do for your heart is play.

---

1 What is the main idea of the passage?
   A How pleasant activities help the heart
   B Why doctors are often misunderstood
   C The ways in which stress causes illness
   D Creating a healthy lifestyle through diet

2 Which of the following conclusions is supported by the information in the passage?
   F Exercise is the single greatest protection against heart disease.
   G The ability to relax and have fun contributes to heart health.
   H It is not easy to counteract day-to-day stress in life.
   J Many people do not know how to maintain a healthy heart.

Test Preparation

UNIT 5 TEST 1

DIRECTIONS
Read the selection. Then answer the questions that follow it.

The Gettysburg Address

"Fourscore and seven years ago . . ." It is an introduction that is known to most Americans whether they can identify its source or not. These are the first five words of arguably one of America's greatest speeches, given by President Abraham Lincoln on November 19, 1863, at the dedication of a National Cemetery. While the power of these few words is tremendous on its own, understanding the context in which the speech was given makes their meaning even deeper and more memorable.

The Battle of Gettysburg was fought from June 30 to July 3, 1863. The Union Army beat the Confederates, but at a very high cost. After four days of fighting, more than 51,000 soldiers were dead, injured, or missing. On November 19 of that year, a National Cemetery in which the lost soldiers of both sides were buried would be dedicated.

Edward Everett, a famous orator of the day, was the keynote speaker. He spoke to the audience for two hours. The president, Abraham Lincoln, was asked to come merely as a formality. He spoke for only two minutes. He spoke simply about the very foundations of American freedom and the sacrifice of the men who lay in the ground. His hope that a "government of the people, by the people, for the people, shall not perish from the earth" is still our greatest hope today.

---

1 Based on the passage, it can be inferred that the author believes which of the following about the Gettysburg Address?
  A It should have been much longer.
  B Its context lessened its impact on the audience.
  C It is an extremely important part of American history.
  D It is not a well-known text in America.

2 What was ironic about Lincoln's address at the time it was given?
  F It did not refer to the battle that had taken place there.
  G It was written by Edward Everett the day before.
  H It was given at the dedication of a National Cemetery.
  J It was not the featured speech on the occasion.

UNIT 5 TEST 2

DIRECTIONS
Read the selection. Then answer the questions that follow it.

A Long Line of Veterans

(1) My ancestors were immigrants, like almost all other Americans. (2) However, unlike many of my friends' families, many of my ancestors were among the first Europeans to set foot on American soil. (3) In fact, this was not even America when they arrived—it was a new land being divided up by several European powers. (4) You see, one-third of my family came to America on the *Mayflower* and claimed Plymouth, Massachusetts for the British Crown. (5) One-third of my family were part of the Native American tribes who were shocked to see Europeans land. (6) The final third of my family left vast Prussian estates behind to find a life in New York City in the 1800s. (5) Altogether, though, a member of my family has fought in every American war from the French and Indian War up through, and including, Vietnam.

(6) There is something special about having a veteran in the family. (7) There is something different in the way we see a former soldier. (8) It is as if their willingness to die for our freedom makes them a part of our lives in a way no other sacrifice can. (9) Any family from any country who has a veteran among them knows this strange and wonderful feeling. (10) Its the knowledge that somehow your entire lineage has made a difference to the world.

---

1 What should be done with the word *were* in sentence 1?
   A Make no change.
   B Delete it.
   C Change it to *being*.
   D Change it to *was*.

2 What should be done to sentence 10?
   F Make no change.
   G Change *Its* to *It's*.
   H Change *somehow* to *someday*.
   J Delete the sentence.

Name _____ Date _____

DIRECTIONS
Read the selection. Then answer the questions that follow it.

Morning

I stretch and lick the momma's face.
Come on, dear mom, pick up the pace.

The momma's moving slow today
I think it must be Saturday.
I'm sitting here and waiting while
She grabs her shoes out of the pile.
I cannot fathom why she's tired.
It's very nearly light outside.

She tries to hitch me up to go
Outside to make my tracks in snow.
But momma's moving far too slow.
Her eyes are falling closed, I know.

She opens up the door, by Gosh,
And I go running like a shot.
I run up to my favorite spot
And sniff and sniff and sniff a lot.

And suddenly, I realize
It's really, really cold outside.
And past the momma's back I fly.
Back into bed I jump and sigh.
It was quite a day I've had.
But why's the momma look so mad?

---

1 What is the poem about?
   A A child who wants to play in the snow
   B A woman trying to get ready for work
   C A dog going for the first walk of the day
   D A holiday morning with family

2 Which best describes the overall tone of the passage?
   F Objective
   G Humorous
   H Passionate
   J Inspiring

UNIT 6 TEST 2

DIRECTIONS
Read the selection. Then answer the questions that follow it.

A Huge Responsibility

Parents: Every holiday season, pet stores are packed with well-meaning moms and dads looking to add a new puppy to the family as a holiday surprise. And every January, shelters are packed with dogs that families found too difficult to care for.

Take time to really consider the time and hard work that goes into raising a new puppy.

1. The Time Commitment: When you get a puppy, you are committing the next ten to fifteen years of your life to caring for another living creature. Your dog will depend on you for food, water, shelter, love, protection, health, and every other need. Consider where you are in your life and whether now is the time to make this commitment.

2. The expense: Your costs do not end when you pay for your puppy. Vaccinations, health visits, accidents, dental cleanings, boarding, grooming, toys, food, beds, etc., consume thousands of dollars over the lifetime of a single dog.

3. The training: Puppies do not enter your home knowing how to sit, roll over, beg, and play catch. In fact, puppies do not enter your home knowing when and where they should take care of their needs. You have to house-train a puppy so it can go outside when it needs to. You need to train it not to bite, not to chew your things, not to get into the garbage or jump on visitors. Teaching a dog is hard work.

Most importantly, if you decide you and your family are ready, please consider adoption over a pet store. There are millions of companion animals at shelters across the country who desperately want a family to love.

---

1 What is the author's purpose in writing this passage?
   A To teach people how to train and care for a puppy
   B To cause people to think carefully before getting a dog
   C To correct the misconception that adopting animals is difficult
   D To stop people from purchasing puppies from pet stores

2 Where are you most likely to find this article?
   F A front-page news article
   G A pet store advertisement
   H An animal shelter newsletter
   J An animal care manual